SW #1470
976.764 17.50

Sanders, Leonard
How Fort Worth Became the
Texas Most City

DATE DUE			

SW
976.764
S

Imperial Public Library
Imperial, Texas

D1788983

HOW FORT WORTH BECAME THE TEXASMOST CITY

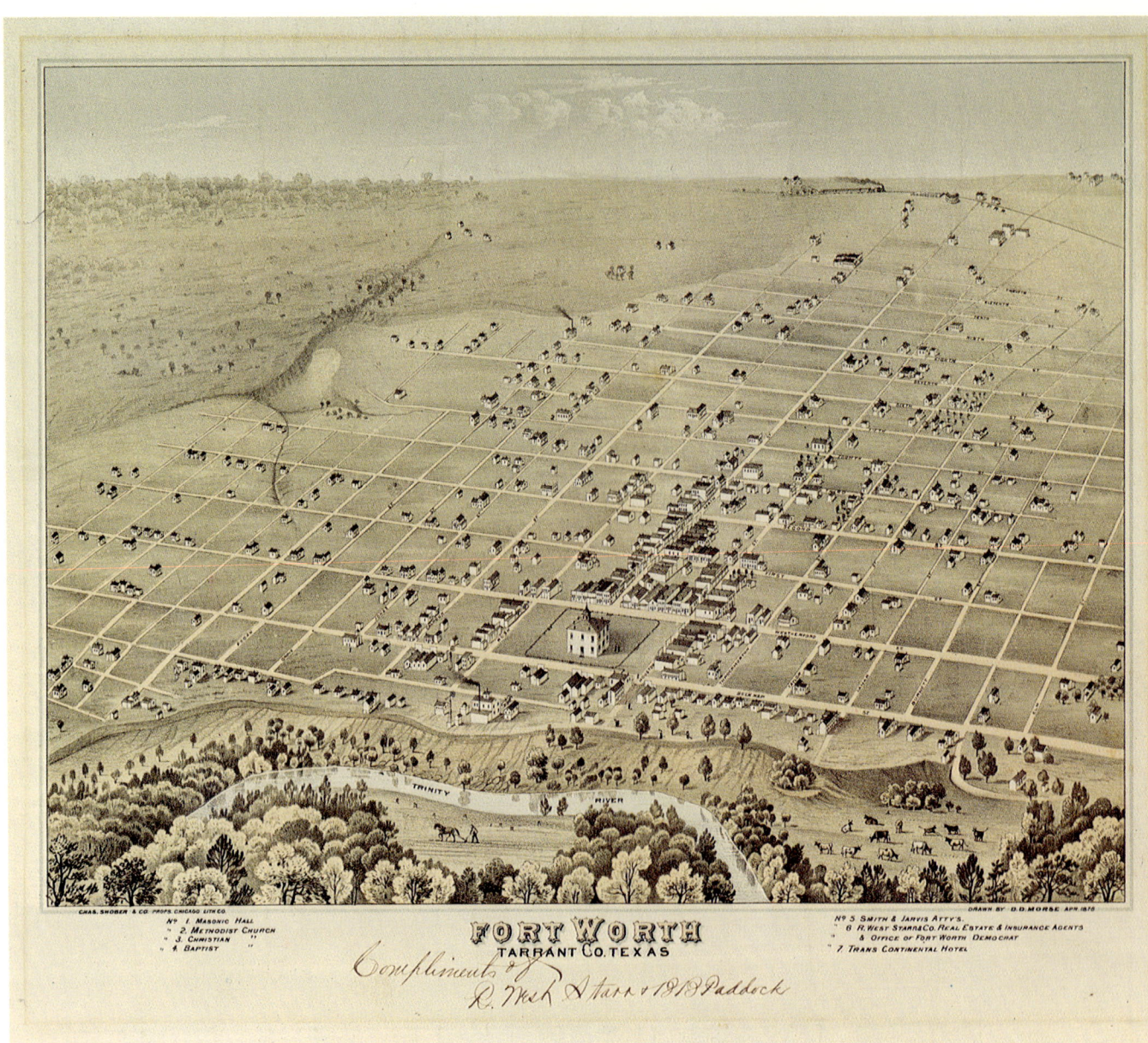

This 1876 view of Fort Worth taken from a drawing by D. D. Morse in April is one of the earliest known views of Fort Worth. It was issued in commemoration of the coming of the railroad, which is shown on the far south side of town, on the horizon. Amon Carter Museum Collection. Gift of Mr. and Mrs. Will F. Collins, Fort Worth

HOW FORT WORTH BECAME THE TEXASMOST CITY

Text by Leonard Sanders
with Captions by Ronnie C. Tyler

Amon Carter Museum of Western Art
Fort Worth

AMON CARTER MUSEUM OF WESTERN ART BOARD OF TRUSTEES
Mrs. J. Lee Johnson III, Chairman
Mrs. Adelyn D. Breeskin
Mrs. Amon G. Carter, Jr.
Amon G. Carter, Jr.
Mrs. Katrine Deakins
John D. Entenza
William H. Goetzmann
Eldridge C. Hanes
Bartlett H. Hayes, Jr.
Sherman E. Lee
C. R. Smith
Mrs. Charles D. Tandy

Mitchell A. Wilder, Director

The Amon Carter Museum was established in 1961 under the will of the late Amon G. Carter for the study and documentation of westering North America. The program of the Museum, expressed in publications, exhibitions, and permanent collections, reflects many aspects of American culture, both historic and contemporary.

LIBRARY OF CONGRESS CATALOG CARD NO. 73-87509 COPYRIGHT © 1973
ISBN 0-88360-002-1
AMON CARTER MUSEUM OF WESTERN ART. ALL RIGHTS RESERVED. LITHOGRAPHY IN USA

PREFACE

An art museum is, of course, concerned with pictures. When this interest is directed to the history of the city in which we live, we become acutely aware of our lack of knowledge of appearances, as distinguished from historic fact. The old city directories make it possible to reconstruct the past with beautifully precise detail—names, addresses, marital status, or economic worth. But we know relatively little of the lives of these alphabetic entries—their fashions, their faces, or their behavior. For this fascinating intelligence we have only the artist and the photographer to assist. Much to our regret, the American West was not an hospitable environment for an artist. We should be the more grateful to those few who did venture onto the frontier to bring home visible documents of the land and the people.

The scarcity of useful pictures grows in almost logarithmic progression as we retreat through the years, and while the popular growth of photography is well recorded in most cities after mid-nineteenth century, the process was poorly adapted to travel and isolated communities. Resident artists and studio photographers did not appear in West Texas until after the Civil War.

Perhaps such evidence of civilization, i.e., image-making, is coincident with the occasion which we identify with this collection of pictures commemorating the centennial of the incorporation of Fort Worth. The city is older than 100 years, but the first two decades saw little more than outpost trading activity. By 1873 life in town had become sufficiently complicated to require more businesslike management of people's lives, hence civic government became formalized in anticipation of further blessings to come.

In 1972 the authors of this book undertook a search of pictorial sources related to Fort Worth and West Texas. In March, 1973, the result of this effort was presented as an exhibition in the Amon Carter Museum of Western Art, marking the one hundredth anniversary of the advent of the city taxpayer. While the authors acknowledge the generous assistance of many collectors and local historians, the Museum and the community are greatly indebted to Ron Tyler and Leonard Sanders for volunteering this publication. Through this effort they have made available the first documented pictorial account of early Fort Worth and have focused attention upon the urgent need for the preservation of local history.

                                                            Mitchell A. Wilder

ACKNOWLEDGMENTS

Many persons aided in the research and preparation of this book. George Younkin, Chief of the Archives Branch of the Federal Archives and Records Center, Region 7, provided both his facilities and advice on methods of research. Dr. Sandra L. Myres, in addition to the invaluable information contained in her annotation of K. M. Van Zandt's autobiography, *Force Without Fanfare,* made available to the authors notes and research material assembled on a parallel project.

Aid on both text and photographs were provided by several members of the staff of the Fort Worth Public Library, including Paul Campbell, Patricia Chadwell, Patricia Weaver and Lydia Herrera. Hettie Arleth, librarian, located and made available material and photographs from the files of the *Fort Worth Star-Telegram.*

Dr. Julia Kathryn Garrett, author of *Fort Worth: A Frontier Triumph,* read the manuscript and offered valuable suggestions, as did Sam B. Cantey III. His support, both in offering suggestions and in providing information and photographs, was encouraging throughout the gestation of the project. Joe Hogsett recalled many interesting facts about Fort Worth in the early 20th century that supplement the captions.

Florene Cooter Sanders read the manuscript in its initial state, and made many invaluable comments on continuity and construction, in addition to her usual contributions of editing and proofreading.

Many persons allowed use of their photographs. They are credited on the page where their photograph appears. Others who offered their material are: Frances M. and Sheila E. Allen, Mr. and Mrs. Will F. Collins, W. P. Cranz, R. B. Lisle, Catherine Terrell McCartney, A. G. McDaniel, Anne McGehearty, Dr. and Mrs. Malcolm D. McLean, Howard G. McPeak, Paul G. Murray, Jim Noah, Dr. W. C.

Nunn, Tom B. Saunders III, all of Fort Worth; Mrs. Wayne Boren of Snyder; John W. Hackney of Midland; Mrs. W. B. Smith of Arlington; Dr. Larkin M. Andrews and Kitty E. Bonno of Houston, and L. M. Riddle of Smithfield.

Several members of the Amon Carter Museum staff provided information and assistance. Mrs. Malcolm D. McLean, microfilm archivist, allowed use of her notes, gleaned over several years of work among the newspapers of Texas. Nancy G. Wynne, librarian, aided in proofreading and editing. Linda Lorenz, photographer, and Glen Pense, assistant photographer, copied literally hundreds of old photographs in preparation for both the exhibition and the book. Marjorie Morey, photographic archivist, spent hours sorting out the prints and matching them with the proper captions. Linda Austin, Karen Dewees and Nancy Ketner prepared the index, and Faythe Taylor typed the final typescript.

L.S.

CONTENTS

  v Preface

vii Acknowledgments

  1 Introduction

  3 I. The Lean Years

 29 II. The Boom Years

 63 III. A Bunch of Wildness

 97 IV. The Good Years

159 V. The Awakening

194 Notes on Sources

199 Bibliography

203 Index

INTRODUCTION

Old photographs conveying a sense of the past inevitably contain something of the forces that have shaped the present. Perhaps this in part explains their timeless appeal.

The pictures in this book, assembled from many sources, reflect life in Fort Worth from the early, lean years of a century ago until the beginning of the second major period of growth at the outbreak of World War I. During these decades, the basic character of Fort Worth was formed.

History often deserves more than mere words. These photographs are invaluable in that their images provide a deeper understanding of the past. In the firm, unyielding faces photographed on Houston Street in the 1870s, we may see considerations that led Major K. M. Van Zandt in 1865 to cast his future with that of Fort Worth. In the direct, no-nonsense portrait of Editor B. B. Paddock, we may gauge the strength of the man who constantly berated, lectured and hounded Fort Worth into living up to its own expectations. In the relaxed scenes at the turn of the century, we sense the contentment of a town engrossed in an enviable pursuit of cultural, educational and personal fulfillment.

The text of this book is not intended as a definitive history of Fort Worth. It focuses on the more significant and colorful events in the hope of analyzing the processes that have evolved Fort Worth's individuality as "the most Texan of Texas cities." A dominant impression emerges: Fort Worth undoubtedly has been affected by a wider variety of the westering experience.

Frank Gruber, the author of scores of western novels and more than 150 western film scripts, once observed that the dramatic form of the western may be reduced to seven basic plots. Most western towns have only two or three examples in their past. To some extent, Fort Worth has experienced all seven elements of western drama. The original fort gave the outpost on the Trinity a sampling of *The Cavalry and Indian Story*. The cattle drives and Fort Worth's long reign as "cowtown" provided *The Ranch Story* and *The Range*

Empire Story. As the hub of railroads and stage lines, Fort Worth was more than conversant with what Gruber termed *The Union Pacific Story*. And Fort Worth's famous trail's-end red light district, Hell's Half Acre, provided ammunition for *The Outlaw Story, The Marshal Story* and *The Revenge Story*.

They all happened here.

Perhaps Fort Worth has been too reticent on certain facets of her past. The truth is that for many decades Fort Worth was one of the liveliest towns in the West. In providing entertainment for Army freighters, buffalo hunters, railroaders and traildrivers, among others, Fort Worth maintained a carefully measured dash of wildness that persisted into the 20th Century.

This long career as "an open town" may seem paradoxical in the face of the steady growth of churches, educational facilities and other cultural outlets. Hell's Half Acre, the target of widespread concern, simply received most of the attention. There may have existed a more biblical understanding of sin and man's fallibility, but Hell's Half Acre was never completely tolerated by the community. Close reading of 19th century newspapers reveals that the forces of reform were strong, and never silent.

Yet, there is evidence that the 24-hour, boom-town vigor of Hell's Half Acre helped to give Fort Worth the daring to accomplish some remarkable feats. Louis L'Amour, the author of more than 50 best-selling western novels based on historical incidents, once observed in conversation that the story of the coming of the railroad to Fort Worth, told herein, is one of the most dramatic he has found in his years of researching the Old West.

Americans long have confused change with progress. Qualities of life well worth preserving are destroyed in the pursuit of momentary goals. Sir Kenneth Clark has defined "a civilisation" as a social structure distinguished by its quality of permanence, evolved by a people who have respect for the past and for the future, and who create works that are meant to endure.

There is little indication that permanence will become the overwhelming preoccupation of our times, but perhaps the popularity of nostalgia in recent years at least signals a recognition that we have abandoned qualities of life worth re-examination. Some of these qualities may be found in these photographs—such as courage and adventure in the early years, ambition and relentless dedication in the boom years, and serenity and a quest for self-fulfillment in the quieter years.

The photographs in this book merit close examination and reflection. In this age of varied life styles, perhaps almost everyone can find something to admire, and to adapt to his own use.

I. THE LEAN YEARS

1. General William Jenkins Worth (1794-1849), hero of the Mexican War, for whom Fort Worth is named. Lithograph by Charles Fenderick. Courtesy Fort Worth Museum of Science and History.

When Brevet Major Ripley Allen Arnold, U. S. Army, first rode into the Trinity River Valley on the afternoon of May 8, 1849, the selection of a site for the founding of Fort Worth was only one of many problems he faced. His orders were plain. He was to establish a military post "somewhere near the confluence of the Clear and West Forks of the Trinity River." He had expert advice in the choice of the exact location. Among his search party was Colonel Middleton Tate Johnson, commander of the Mounted Texas Volunteers in Federal Service at Johnson Station.[1] After two years in the region, Johnson knew the country better than anyone else with the exception of the Indians.

Simon B. Ferrar, a member of Johnson's Company, later recalled the day Fort Worth was founded:

> After staying about a week at Johnson Station, we started in company with Major Arnold and command up Trinity River in search of a place to locate the regular United States troops. We passed through the Cross-Timbers, crossing the different creeks as best we could, through a wild and beautiful country inhabited only by Indians, wild or mustang horses, innumerable quantities of deer, wolves and wild turkeys.

The group halted early in the afternoon and killed a deer for supper. They camped that night at Cold Springs.[2] The next morning, Major Arnold and Colonel Johnson climbed the bluffs to the southwest and from that vantage point selected a site for the future fort.[3] On flat land in a bend of the river, the location offered a plentiful supply of good water.

This was the beginning of a lonely outpost on the Texas frontier, and the start of Major Arnold's troubles. With a single company of U. S. Dragoons, he had been given the almost impossible job of keeping the peace along a two-hundred-mile frontier. The reward for success would be survival.

Reports had persisted for years that there were Indian encampments of as many as two thousand warriors on the upper reaches of the Trinity and

Brazos Rivers. The reported locations of these villages varied. General Edward H. Tarrant, Colonel Edward Burleson and other early Indian fighters had failed to find them. Doubts were voiced in Texas newspapers that the villages existed. The point was moot. Evidence abounded that there were plenty of hostile Indians. Hardly a month went by without a new account to add to the long history of Indian depredations in Texas.[4]

The hostile Indians, most notably the Comanches and Kiowas, seemed to have a sixth sense for catching Texans engrossed in their own troubles. During the Texas War for Independence, the Indians raided to the Gulf, wiping out such early Texas outposts as Fort Parker. After Texans won Independence from Mexico in 1836, the impoverished Republic of Texas was forced to focus most of its slim defense along the southern border against the expected renewal of hostilities with Mexico. Throughout the late 1830s and early 1840s, the tide of settlement in North Texas retreated under repeated assaults from the Plains Indians. Then, along with statehood in 1845, there came the long-anticipated Mexican War. Not until its conclusion in 1848 was attention again turned to the protection of the Northwest frontier.

The population in North Texas was huddled around scattered settlements. Jonathan Bird's Fort, established in 1840 on the Trinity, sheltered a community of fifty persons. Twenty-five miles downstream, John Neely Bryan's Trading Post, established in the same year, had grown into a community of three hundred called Dallas. The Peters Land Company had established its headquarters near Dallas, at Farmers Branch, and a few Peters colonists had settled as far west as the Grapevine Prairie in a community called Lonesome Dove.

Other efforts at settlement had ended in failure. Two Arkansas traders, Ed Terrell and John P. Lusk, attempted to establish a post on the Clear Fork of the Trinity in 1844. They felled and trimmed logs for a fort, but were seized by Indians before its completion. They spent a year in captivity before talking and trading their way to freedom.[5]

Statehood shifted the burden of protection to Federal hands. In January of 1849, General William Jenkins Worth arrived in San Antonio to take command of the Eighth and Ninth Military Departments, which encompassed Texas and New Mexico. A hero of the War of 1812, Worth was nearing the end of a long career. He was a former commandant at West Point, and was credited as being the field tactician who ended the Seminole Indian Wars. Diaries and journals indicate that he was one of the most popular generals in the Mexican War. His admirers felt that he, not General Zachary Taylor, deserved the laurels for the American victory at Monterrey. In the "War of the Generals" for acclaim after the capture of Mexico City, Worth insisted that it was he, not General Winfield Scott, who had chosen the successful route around Lake Chalco. His charge received considerable support.

For the protection of North Texas, Worth proposed the establishment of a line of forts just to the west of San Antonio, Austin, Waco Village and Dallas. Worth named Brevet Major Ripley Allen Arnold to command the two northernmost forts. The choice was no accident.

At 32, Arnold had much experience; he had served under Worth in the Florida and Mexico campaigns. A graduate of West Point, he twice won battlefield promotions in the Seminole War. He arrived in Texas with the Army of Occupation after statehood in 1845, and was sent into Mexico with the outbreak of the war. For his leadership in the two opening battles, he was breveted major. Later, he was named assistant quartermaster, with the responsibility of a long supply line into Mexico.

But the founding of forts was something new in Arnold's experience.

After locating the site for his northernmost outpost, he returned to the old Towash village west of Waco Village where he had established a post to be known as Fort Graham. There he learned that General Worth had died of cholera in San Antonio. Arnold named his new outpost Camp Worth in honor of his dead commander.[6]

Leaving Company I, half his command, at Fort Graham, Arnold returned to Camp Worth with Company F on June 6, 1849. He asked that his mail be forwarded to "Dallas, Dallas County, Texas, a town about thirty-five miles east of me."[7]

Arnold was deeply disturbed by his precarious situation. He soon made his concern known. On June 15, 1849, he wrote directly to his new commanding officer, General William S. Harney: "I am building a new post at this place (the extreme northern frontier yet occupied) and my company is so small that I cannot keep up my scouting parties."

He noted that this information had been brought to the attention of his regimental commander. He remained eloquently silent on the point that he still was awaiting results. He asked if there were "any drilled recruits" at the Cavalry Depot. He added: "Those assigned me... in November last with one exception had not even been drilled in the Carbine Manual or Saber Exercises or at least knew nothing of them."

Four days later, he submitted to the adjutant general in Washington a full roster of his command, with pertinent commentary. He noted that while the authorized Company F strength was three officers and 86 enlisted men, he could field only three sergeants, four corporals and 25 privates fit for duty. He was the only commissioned officer.

He pointed out that "this is not a mere morning report but the roll of my entire company." His comments revealed something of his mood. One private was listed as "saddler, and always at work at old equipment." Another was deemed "perfectly worthless. Can't trust him with horse or equipment."

Yet, Arnold was quick to jump to the defense of his men. Less than three weeks after Camp Worth was established, Arnold wrote Army headquarters in Washington to refute published rumors that the Dragoons under his command at Camp Worth and Fort Graham had lost horses to the Indians:

> I have the honor to contradict such a report and to state that the two companies of Dragoons which have been under my command have not had a horse stolen since their arrival in Texas in November last nor have I heard of any Indian depredations committed in this part of the country for several months. About one hundred Indians of the different wild tribes are now visiting me. They brought down and delivered up some thirty-five horses which they had taken from the Wichitas, horses stolen within the last year from citizens. Three Wichita chiefs are here and promise everything for the future. All is peace and quiet on this frontier.

The qualms Arnold may have felt for his small, untrained command apparently were not shared by most Texans. On July 13, 1849, the Marshall *Texas Republican* published an editorial in praise of Arnold and his men:

> We are gratified to learn that the Dragoons stationed between the Brazos and Trinity, under the command of Captain Arnold, have proved themselves to be fully as efficient as the Rangers that proceeded [sic] them. During the period that they have been stationed on the Brazos, the settlers have enjoyed a complete immunity from Indian depredations . . . . These treacherous savages have their haunts in the Wichita mountains of Arkansas [territory], and have been in the habit of making forays into the settlements between the Trinity and the Brazos. Nothing but the fear that the Dragoons would carry fire and sword through the villages could have induced them to sue for peace . . . . We learn that Captain Arnold intends to remove his camp [sic] . . . to a large and beautiful spring of clear wholesome water. The country around the spring is exceedingly fertile and abounds in excellent pasturage. It will doubtless become the seat of extensive and flourishing settlements.

The newspaper article was prophetic; Arnold soon was presented with a new concern. With the increased protection, a steady parade of what he termed "citizen gentlemen" passed through the camp on their way west to scout commercial prospects. As an officer and fellow gentleman, Arnold repeatedly found himself in the role of host. His 60 dollars a month as brevet major was supplemented by a four-dollar ration allowance. Arnold found that this was not enough. He wrote to the War Department, asking an additional four dollars a month to cover this unexpected expense.

Arnold was given reason for second thoughts on the location of his post. Although selected because of its access to Cold Springs, the site in late July received too much water. A Trinity flood sent the Dragoons to higher ground; Camp Worth was moved to the top of the bluff.[8]

A settler, John Press Farmer, and his wife and daughter were living in a tent on the new site. A native of Tennessee, Farmer had sampled East Texas for two years before moving westward to the Trinity in 1849. He and his wife had cut some timber, and their home was almost completed when Indians were sighted. The Farmers fled on horseback. When they returned, their home was charred rubble.

An amicable compromise was made for the Army's use of the Farmer campsite. Farmer was appointed post sutler. He became Fort Worth's first permanent civilian resident.[9]

The Army's response to Major Arnold's plea for more men was slow. Thirty-nine enlisted men and two officers of Company F, Eighth Infantry, arrived on October 6. Eighteen recruits and an officer arrived on Christmas Day to fill in the Dragoon company ranks. With the new men, work progressed more rapidly on the construction of the fort, and Arnold at last was able to establish a system of patroling the region.

Two other events raised hopes for the permanence of the outpost. On November 14, the Army gave the camp the official designation of "Fort Worth." On December 20, the creation of Tarrant County from the northern portion of Navarro was signed into law by Governor George T. Wood. In naming Tarrant County, the Third Legislature honored a man who had worked hard in its behalf, General Edward H. Tarrant, a veteran Indian fighter and a representative from Navarro and Limestone Counties.

The most populous community in the new country was Birdville, which had formed in the vicinity of Bird's Fort. It became the county seat.

Fort Worth was virtually completed by midwinter. Most of the labor was provided by the troopers. They erected three sets of officers' quarters, an earthen-floor log barracks sufficient for 120 men, a hospital and dispensary, stables, a commissary store, a guard house, and a quartermaster storehouse.

Not everyone shared Major Arnold's opinion on fort design. Lieutenant William H. C. Whiting, an engineer who visited Fort Worth shortly after its completion, sent in a critical report:

> The fort has been laid out on a scale rather contracted — probably as designed originally but for one company. And the arrangement of the stables I cannot commend: they are much too near the quarters of both officers and men, and, however thorough the police may be, cannot but be offensive in summer.

Despite the fort's limited facilities, the number of visiting "citizen gentlemen" increased. Some elected to stay. They found home sites and settled near the fort. Archibald F. Leonard and Henry Daggett became partners in a civilian store, located in a grove to the northeast of the fort to comply with Army regulations that did not allow a civilian business within one mile of a military post.

The fort's closest brush with extensive military action came in the following summer. A wandering group of Tonkawas was attacked by other Indians just to the west of the fort. Identified as mixed Comanches and Caddos, the hostile Indians outnumbered the Tonkawas. Estimates of the Comanche-Caddo force, believed to be under the command of Chief Towash, ranged as high as six hundred warriors. Major Arnold and his men watched the battle. In the opening clash, several warriors on each side were killed or wounded.

During a lull in the battle, the Tonkawas sent a messenger to the fort, asking protection. On Arnold's order, a lieutenant and a small detachment rode out and escorted the Tonkawas to safety. Arnold granted them refuge in the commissary quarters.

Abe Harris, sergeant-major of the post's infantry company, described subsequent events:

> Here came Towash and five or six hundred of his warriors, in high rage that their game had been spoiled, and demanding that the refugees be surrendered immediately. During the first year or so after these posts were established on the frontier, the Indians were very presumptuous because of their great superiority in numbers and were confident they could wipe out the entire establishment whenever they got ready. Well, when Towash sent in his ultimatum to the effect that he would attack the garrison if his enemies were not given up, Major Arnold told him to come on. The Major directed that the one howitzer at the post should be loaded and fired at a door set up at considerable distance. When the shell went whizzing past the Indians and exploded so as to blow the wooden target into a thousand pieces they needed no further argument to satisfy them that they didn't want a fight. Their belligerent attitude vanished, and Indian like, the next instant they were begging for something to eat. Major Arnold told them he would just as soon fight them as feed them, but nevertheless had three beeves driven out to them. Those savages were certainly more hungry than hostile, for the next morning there was neither hide, hair nor hoof of those devoted cattle to be seen. And this was the peaceful outcome of the only hostilities Fort Worth ever experienced.[10]

The post gradually assumed a different atmosphere. In the summer of 1850, Arnold's wife and children arrived from Washington. They brought the first piano to Fort Worth. The presence of women on post, and of children playing on the parade ground, altered the flavor of camp life. For Major Arnold, the next few years should have been an idyllic interlude in his military career. Instead, they were filled with tragedy.

First, the Arnolds' two younger children, Sophie and Willis, died shortly after their arrival at the post. They were buried near the fort, in Pioneer Rest Cemetery.

In the following year, Arnold returned to Fort Graham to attend to some political problems there. On September 6, 1853, he was killed in a quarrel with the post surgeon, Dr. Josephus M. Steiner.

Arnold had broken up an argument the evening before between Steiner and a drunken lieutenant. Arnold gave both a night's rest and a chance for sober reflection. He then issued an order for their arrest. When Steiner received the arrest order, he threw it down, brushed his escort aside, and went straight to Arnold's quarters. After a heated verbal exchange, both drew pistols. Arnold fired twice, but missed. His gun malfunctioned on the third shot. Steiner shot Arnold four times. The major died a few minutes later.

His body was returned to Fort Worth the following year and reinterred in Pioneer Rest Cemetery near the graves of his two children. Masonic rites were conducted at his graveside, the first ever to be held in Fort Worth.

Many changes occurred during Arnold's brief career in Fort Worth. The frontier moved almost a hundred miles westward. A new line of forts was established. On September 17, 1853, Fort Worth was abandoned. The Fort Worth garrison was ordered to move westward to Fort Belknap.

If the departing troops had burned the post's crude buildings, Fort Worth might have faded into history. But in that era, shelter was at a premium. The settlers were quick to take advantage of the unexpected windfall.

Daggett and Leonard moved their mercantile store into the rough but spacious barracks. A trader, Julian B. Feild, opened a competing store in one of the officers' quarters.

Many new settlers arrived. One, John Peter Smith, an unusually talented young man, started Fort Worth's first school in 1854. A graduate of Bethany College in Virginia, he was versed in Greek, Latin and the classics. His riches for the most part were cerebral; he came west on foot, walking most of the way from Kentucky. He hitched a ride with a wagon train to Dallas, and set out walking to Fort Worth. He was given a ride the last five miles.

Two of Henry Daggett's brothers, C. B. and Eph, came to Fort Worth in 1854. Captain Eph, celebrated for his exploits in the Mexican War, converted the Army stables into Fort Worth's first hotel. As a conversation piece, the hotel housed Santa Anna's personal silver washbasin, captured by Captain Eph on a day when he narrowly missed capturing the general.

In that same year, Fort Worth's first civilian physician arrived. Dr. Carroll M. Peak, who had been practicing in Dallas a short time, came to Fort Worth to attend Julian Feild during an illness. Dr. Peak was impressed with the prospects of the new community. He stayed. Colonel Nathaniel Terry, a former lieutenant governor of Alabama, arrived and erected a plantation-style home near Cold Springs. J. C. Terrell, a young lawyer, was on his way to the California gold fields when he came through Fort Worth to visit a friend and colleague, Dabney C. Dade. Terrell and Dade became law partners. A well-equipped wagon train arrived with a number of residents from Dodd County, Kentucky. Leaving crowded conditions and exhausted land in Kentucky, the new arrivals hoped to get a fresh start. They settled to the west of Fort Worth in a community that came to be known as White Settlement. Many of the planters brought slaves.

Fort Worth grew rapidly and soon rivaled Birdville in population.

The commercial aspects of "county seat" status and "court Monday" were not to be dismissed lightly. In 1856 Fort Worth managed to wrangle the issue of the county seat onto the ballot in a special election.

The campaign was fierce and, from Fort Worth's standpoint, well-planned. Fort Worth enthusiasts made certain that on election day Birdville had no keg of free whiskey, and that Fort Worth had two barrels. On the night before the election, a group from Fort Worth siphoned off Birdville's hidden supply of whiskey and brought it to Fort Worth. It was dispensed free on election day.

There were other election irregularities. Voters came from the farthest reaches of the county. Some faces were not well-known. Although Press Farmer's father-in-law, Sam Woody, cast his vote for Fort Worth, he happened to be a resident of Wise County. Woody thoughtfully brought along 14 neighbors, who also voted. Fort Worth won the county seat by seven votes.

A feud between the two towns, generated principally in that election, flared into violence on several occasions. Fort Worth lawyer A. Y. Fowler and Birdville supporter Hiram Calloway traded hot words at a celebration at Cold Springs. During the dispute, Calloway pushed Fowler, who tumbled off a cliff and broke an arm. Fowler felt that the peacemaking efforts of Tarrant County Sheriff John B. York were slanted toward Calloway. Fowler later met York on the street. Both drew pistols and fired. Both died.

Three Fort Worth supporters, Jack Brinson, George Slaughter, and Tom Johnson, tangled with a Birdville supporter named Tucker in 1856. Tucker was killed.

Perhaps the most unusual shooting to arise out of the dispute occurred in Birdville. John J. Courtney, editor of the *Birdville Western Express,* founded in 1855 as Tarrant County's first newspaper, was a man of strong opinions. He published them regularly, and some did not find agreement among his readers. He was an early advocate of secession. He also believed that Fort Worth should be the county seat. The editor of the *Birdville Union,* A. G. Walker, was equally ardent for Birdville and the Union. Their editorial battle, long waged in printer's ink, ended in hot lead. Walker killed Courtney in a gun battle on the streets of Birdville.

Communication and transportation between Fort Worth and the world improved as the population increased. A post office was opened on February 28, 1856, with Julian Feild as postmaster. Lawrence Steele built a two-story hotel which he named "Steele's Tavern."[11] On July 18, 1856, the first licensed stagecoach arrived; fare was purchased at Steele's Tavern, which provided a parlor and a sitting room for the ladies.

The increased communication helped to make the era's heated political issues a matter of even more local concern. Sam Houston, running for governor as a Jackson Democrat or Unionist, brought his bitter, unsuccessful campaign to Tarrant County in 1857, stirring still greater interest. He met Louis T. Wigfall, a supporter of Democratic candidate Hardin R. Runnels, in a debate at Birdville. Most of Fort Worth attended. Afterward, Houston accepted the invitation of Captain Eph Daggett to spend the night in Fort Worth.[12] Daggett, a slave owner, was not a Houston supporter. His invitation was a measure of his esteem for the aging hero of San Jacinto.

The hardships of one of Texas' most vicious political campaigns were wearing on Houston's health. The ankle wound he received at San Jacinto was bothering him, and his limp was more pronounced. The near-fatal abdominal wound he received in his youth at Horseshoe Bend, while serving with Andrew Jackson, remained open and required fresh dressings each day throughout his life. Daggett brought out Santa Anna's silver washbowl to use in bathing the wound.

Houston's pro Union stand was no more popular in Tarrant County than in other sections of Texas. Many residents owned slaves, and the number was increasing. In the spring of 1855, a 525-foot cedar log bridge, the largest in Texas, was completed across the Trinity at Dallas. A newspaper reported that during a five-month period, an average of ten or fifteen immigrant wagons crossed the bridge daily, bound for settlement on the upper reaches of the Trinity. The newspaper observed:

> The immigrants are generally men of wealth, their families traveling in carriages. They are chiefly from Tennessee, Kentucky and Missouri, and

bring their Negroes with them. The amount of immigrants is considerably more than last year. Lands are rapidly appreciating in value. Unimproved lands now sell at from $2 to $5 per acre; while lands under some improvements bring from $8 to $10 per acre.

Slaves represented a considerable investment. On January 7, 1854, the Marshall *Texas Republican* reported:

On Monday and Tuesday last were the days for the annual sales and the hiring of property, and our streets were crowded with people. Negroes were sold at what we consider to be very high prices. Ordinary Negro men sold for from fifteen to eighteen hundred dollars; Negro women from a thousand to twelve hundred. Negro men (ordinary field hands) hired from $235 to $312. Women at from $140 to $170; in these cases the hirer paying for clothing. The natural inference would be that a country must be very productive when people can afford to pay such prices for labor.

Fort Worth's principal slave owner was Colonel Nathaniel Terry, with thirty-six blacks. Paul Isbell, Charles Turner and Captain Eph Daggett also owned a number of slaves. Yet, the pro-slavery sentiment in Fort Worth stemmed more from principle than practice; most states-righters did not own slaves. In effect, their stand was nearer to "anti-abolitionist" than "pro-slavery."

The issues that brought about the Civil War came to a reckoning early in North Texas. As early as 1856, rumors of slave insurrections were widely circulated. Frank Leslie's *Illustrated Newspaper* reported on October 4, 1856, that an insurrectionist plot involving four hundred Negroes had been discovered at Columbus, Texas:

The Negroes intended to commence their operations tomorrow, and would probably have completed their design, had not a slave belonging to a Mr. Toake informed his master of the fact . . . . A number of the Negroes were in custody, and some two or three were to be hanged today. One was whipped so severely that he afterwards died. Two or three Mexicans were arrested who were supposed to be instigators of the insurrection. The Negroes had a large quantity of arms and ammunition secreted, and everything necessary to render them formidable.

In the summer of 1859, Sam Houston again brought his campaign for governor to Fort Worth. He met Governor Hardin Runnels in a debate at Cold Springs in a Fourth of July celebration. Also on the program were barbecue, watermelon, and a Grand Tournament.[13] Houston was a guest in the home of Colonel Nathaniel Terry. Governor Runnels traveled on to Johnson Station to spend the night.

Houston won the election despite his pro-Union views. His Indian policy helped. After several trouble-free years, Indians again were raiding deep into

Texas, and the U.S. Army seemed helpless. Houston proposed the raising of 25 volunteers from each county to supplement the Texas Rangers in stopping the depredations. The plan was extremely popular. Texas had developed the habit of turning to Houston in troubled times.

The period of growing unrest was not eased by a renewal of the Fort Worth-Birdville feud. The Legislature was still receiving heated complaints in Austin concerning the 1856 election. Sentiment was high for another balloting.

Following the adage that possession is 11 points in the law, 38 Fort Worth residents pledged to pay from their own pockets the total cost of a permanent courthouse. They hoped that the prospect of no additional taxes would help Fort Worth's cause.

Fort Worth now had a numerical edge over Birdville. The Fort Worth-Jacksboro Stage Line had gone into operation in 1858, making connections with the Butterfield Overland Stage to the West Coast and to St. Louis. Steele's Tavern became a popular overnight stop. Passengers were escorted to Fort Worth's principal attraction, the "view from the bluff." Some stayed. Others spread word of Fort Worth's prospects far and wide. The population grew steadily.

Fort Worth won the 1860 county-seat election, polling 548 votes. An undesignated "center of the county" received 301; Birdville polled only four votes.

Work was started immediately on a stone courthouse to fulfill Fort Worth's pledge.

News reports of the Abe Lincoln-Stephen Douglas debates in Illinois, Harriet Beecher Stowe's continued inflammatory writings in the wake of *Uncle Tom's Cabin,* and repeated rumors of abolitionist plots kept Fort Worth's political scene in ferment. The town's first newspaper, the *Fort Worth Chief,* helped to set the stage for violence.

The founder of the *Chief,* Anthony Banning Norton, was a radical in every sense of the word. A native of Ohio and a lawyer, Norton had campaigned for Henry Clay in the 1844 presidential race against James K. Polk. When Clay lost, Norton did not accept defeat gracefully. "The country might be going to hell but I'm going to Texas," he said, paraphrasing David Crockett. He vowed not to cut his hair or trim his beard until Henry Clay was elected president.

When he arrived in Fort Worth five years later, he was a sight to be remembered. Soon after launching the *Chief,* he left Editor George Smith in charge and moved to Austin, where he founded the *Austin Intelligencer.* He continued to file his pro-Union, abolitionary views to the *Chief* by mail.

On July 8, 1860, the abolitionist issue flared beyond a mere abstraction for Tarrant County. More than half the buildings fronting the square in Dallas were burned; the loss was placed at four hundred thousand dollars. Denton, Pilot Point, Austin, Waxahachie and other Texas towns were victims of fires on the same afternoon. Archibald Leonard's flour mill, just east of Fort Worth, went up in flames.[14]

Retaliation was swift. Dallas citizens hanged three Negroes, and appointed a committee to whip every Negro in the county. In their final moments, the condemned blacks implicated two white preachers from the North.

Most communities in the South at the time harbored a vigilante committee of secret membership; Fort Worth was no exception. The Tarrant County committee apparently was successful in thwarting a plot brewing in Fort Worth. An abolitionist, otherwise unidentified, was hanged from a pecan tree on the Clear Fork just west of town.[15] Fifty pistols and a batch of strychnine were found among slaves.

On August 10, 1860, Paul Isbell, a slave owner and trader from White Settlement, brought in a letter found on his farm. Couched in evangelistic terms, the letter praised the work of the "Mystic Red," identified as a secret order of Union incendiaries. Outlined was a plan to create havoc in Texas in order to link the Great Lakes and the Gulf, "to surround slavery by land and water."

The letter created a furor in Fort Worth. In a mass meeting on the public square, Fort Worth citizens adopted five resolutions. The first decreed that everyone connected with the crimes had placed themselves "beyond the pale." The second provided for two lists, one of suspected Black Republicans, who should be watched, and a "Black List" of those who should be hanged immediately. The third resolution said, in effect, that anyone who did not concur belonged on one list or the other. The fourth resolution said there would be no exceptions. The fifth resolution declared that everyone who attributed the recent fires to accident—persons such as Editor Norton—should be placed on the first list.

The resolutions were soon tested. Two itinerant bricklayers from the North were found to be talking with Negroes in Tarrant County's small slave churches. A loyal slave, Ned Purvis, was induced to hide under the floor of a church during a meeting. He reported that the two Yankees were urging a slave uprising. One of the men, Anthony Bewley, escaped. He was soon captured and returned to Fort Worth. On September 13, 1860, Bewley and his companion, a Mr. Crawford[16], were hanged from Fort Worth's hanging tree. As a warning to other abolitionists the bodies were left swinging until reduced to skeletons.

A grand jury in session at Weatherford, Parker County, made official observation of these events. Although the members acknowledged that the matter was outside their purview, they commended Fort Worth's actions, and suggested that Editor Norton should also be hanged.

Two months later, Abraham Lincoln was elected President. Anti-Union sentiment continued to mount. But the issues were complex. There were those who supported slavery, but opposed secession. There were those who had no strong opinions on slavery, or perhaps opposed it, but who endorsed secession on principle. Many felt that Texas should "go it alone" once again by shunning both the Union and the Confederacy.

In another public meeting, Fort Worth residents adopted a resolution urging Governor Houston to assemble the Legislature. They also voted to raise the Lone Star Flag in Fort Worth "as the banner of our liberties." Cooler heads—notably John Peter Smith, Colonel Johnson, and Captain Daggett—carefully worded the resolution to imply that the act was not one of actual secession.

A secessionist convention in Austin passed an ordinance on February 1, 1861, to quit the Union. The matter was subject to a popular vote.

Tarrant County's dilemma was evident in the balloting on February 23; secession carried the county by only 27 votes out of 800 polled. No doubt many remembered the words of Sam Houston shortly before the election:

> "Some of you laugh to scorn the idea of bloodshed as the result of secession. But let me tell you what is coming . . .
>
> Your fathers and husbands, your sons and brothers, will be herded at the point of the bayonet . . .
>
> You may, after the sacrifice of countless millions of treasure and hundreds of thousands of lives, as a bare possibility, win Southern independence . . . but I doubt it.

In Austin, Houston ignored the secessionist convention. He said he would deal only with the legally constituted Legislature, which was not in session. When he failed to answer the convention roll call, the office of governor was declared vacant. At the time, Houston was seated on the south porch of the Executive Mansion a short distance away. A passerby brought him the news. "Texas is lost," Houston said to his wife

When war came, Fort Worth bore its share of economic chaos, privations, Indian raids and deaths, both at home and in the ranks.

Ten companies of volunteers left Tarrant County for Confederate service. The first, Company A, Ninth Texas Cavalry Regiment commanded by William Quayle of Grapevine, departed on August 20, 1861. Colonel Johnson, although an opponent of secession, organized a brigade, and later supervised a fleet of blockade-runners. John Peter Smith, another opponent of secession, helped to raise a company under Captain Thomas A. Moody, and marched off to fight for the South. Captain M. J. Brinson organized Company D, Ninth Texas Cavalry Regiment.

In addition, others joined the Frontier Guard to take over protection of the settlers to the northwest. Parker, Jack, Palo Pinto, Clay, Montague, Wise, Cooke, and Young Counties suffered under repeated Indian depredations. Attempts to corral the Indians were without success. In October of 1860 the *Dallas Herald* reported:

> By private letters from Weatherford we learn that about thirty of Col. M. T. Johnson's men came from Belknap a few days since, foot-back and a-walking, half starved. Some of them stated they had subsisted several days on what they could pick up by the way, and most of them were barefooted. Their horses were stolen by the Indians and even the blankets pilfered. Rumor has it that out of sixty-five horses fifty-nine were stolen or stampeded, and the company was left without provisions ninety miles in the wilderness beyond Belknap.

One effort at retaliation was successful. Captain Lawrence Sullivan Ross was named to organize an expedition into Comanche country. With 70 Texas Rangers, volunteers, and a detachment of the U.S. Second Cavalry, Ross battled a band of Comanches on the Pease River. One captive was identified as Cynthia Ann Parker, stolen by the Comanches in a raid on Fort Parker in 1836, when she was nine years of age. Cynthia Ann and her daughter, Prairie Flower, were returned to their uncle, Isaac Parker, who took her to the family home near Birdville. In passing through Fort Worth in 1862, Cynthia Ann and her baby were taken by A. F. Corning to a daguerreotype gallery, where her picture was made. She later was taken to live with the family of another uncle, Silas Parker, in Van Zandt County. She was never able to forget Indian ways or her Indian family, husband Peta Nocona and son Quanah Parker. After the death of Prairie Flower in 1864, Cynthia Ann pined away and died.

Under repeated Indian raids and the hardships of wartime, the line of settlement in North Texas retreated drastically. In 1861 a Young County resident wrote:

> There must be a frontier at some point. To the north and northwest of us lies a belt of country from fifty to one hundred miles in width, once settled by an enterprising and industrious people, but who have been compelled to recede before the overpowering savages and have fallen back, at each step letting them in nearer to you, and when and where shall this retro-migration cease?

Fort Worth was given reason for to ponder the question. Tarrant County's population dropped from an estimated six thousand to approximately one thousand. Fort Worth itself dwindled to a population near 250. As the war raged through four long years, those who remained in Fort Worth could only wait, and endure.

NOTES, THE LEAN YEARS

1. Johnson's Station, located on Marrow Bone or Mary le Bone Creek three miles south of Arlington, was established in 1847. His fort-home provided a sorghum mill, gristmill, blacksmith shop, a store, and a business and a social center, as well as protection, for the surrounding region.

2. Cold Springs, which became a recreation and picnic center for Fort Worth in the early days, is located just east of where Cold Springs Road today spans the Trinity River northeast of the Courthouse.

3. Initially, the fort was located between today's Courthouse, and Cold Springs.

4. "Depredations" was an eloquent 19th century term in common use. A reader who delves into primary sources soon finds that Indians seldom "raided;" they "committed depredations." "Depredation claims" were filed against the government to recover the cost of stolen and destroyed property.

5. "We finally worked our rabbit's foot and the Indians turned us loose," Captain Ed Terrell said just before his death at the age of 93 in 1905. "We then lost no time in leaving this section, and I did not return until 1849, when the troops were stationed here. . . . It was either a case of leaving Tarrant County—or what is now Tarrant County—or losing our scalps, and when a man lost his hair in those days he generally lost something else . . . In those days this country was infested with Indians and herds of buffalo were all around us. There were more panthers in these parts than I have ever seen before or since; antelopes without number, wild turkeys in every tree—in fact, in those days this was God's own country."

6. The designation of "Fort Worth" also was given to one of the defenses of Washington, D. C., during the Civil War. It was located about three miles west of Alexandria, Virginia. A "Camp Worth" was located in Tennessee in 1836. Neither designation survived. Lake Worth, Florida, also was named for General Worth.

7. Twentieth century readers may appreciate this precedent.

8. The fort buildings were on the land immediately west of today's Courthouse, now bounded by Bluff and Weatherford, Houston and Throckmorton.

9. Press Farmer's daughter Sue, born in 1852, was the first white child born in Fort Worth. Howard W. Peak, born in 1856 to Dr. and Mrs. Carroll M. Peak, was the first boy.

10. The Plains Indians never had much use for Tonkawas. The Comanche name for them was "neuma-takers," which means "eaters of human flesh." The Kiowas called them "kia-hi-piago," which means the same thing. In the fall of 1862, after an alleged act of cannibalism, the Comanches, Caddos and Kiowas joined forces in an effort to exterminate the Tonkawas, and came close to success in a massacre southeast of present-day Anadarko, Oklahoma. The few survivors fled to Texas forts for protection. Later, a handful of Tonkawas obtained some measure of revenge by serving as scouts for Colonel Ranald S. Mackenzie in his final, relentless campaign against the Plains Indians in the 1870s.

11. Lawrence Steele imported a bell that became one of Fort Worth's oldest relics. Cast in 1782, the bell was used as the hotel dinner bell and—by extension—the town's first alarm system. Today the bell is housed in the Masonic Temple.

12. Daggett's home was between Main and Houston, and Tenth and Eleventh Streets.

13. This refers to a fad in the Old West generally ignored by Hollywood. The object was to lance a series of dangling rings while riding at full tilt. The contest was replete with courtly gestures and conduct toward opponents and, most especially, the ladies. Winners were accorded impressive titles loosely adapted from days of yore. On September 3, 1868, the *San Antonio Daily Herald* commented: "Tournaments in Texas are becoming as numerous as barbecues... we heartily approve of both, for we believe that none but Democrats participate in these gatherings."

14. Archibald Leonard's flour mill, the first in the area, was a community center where news was exchanged and goods traded while farmers waited for their grain to be ground. The mill was rebuilt, and later was owned by W. A. Randol. The road past the mill later became Randol Mill Road.

15. Some local historians believe that this tree, which had further use, was located about three hundred yards west of the Jacksboro Highway (Henderson Street)-White Settlement Road intersection. Others place it closer to White Settlement. Another well known hanging tree was at the foot of Samuels Avenue, where the street dips into the lowlands.

16. Apparently no one bothered to remember Crawford's given name. It does not survive. Anthony Bewley's name in some references is spelled "Buley."

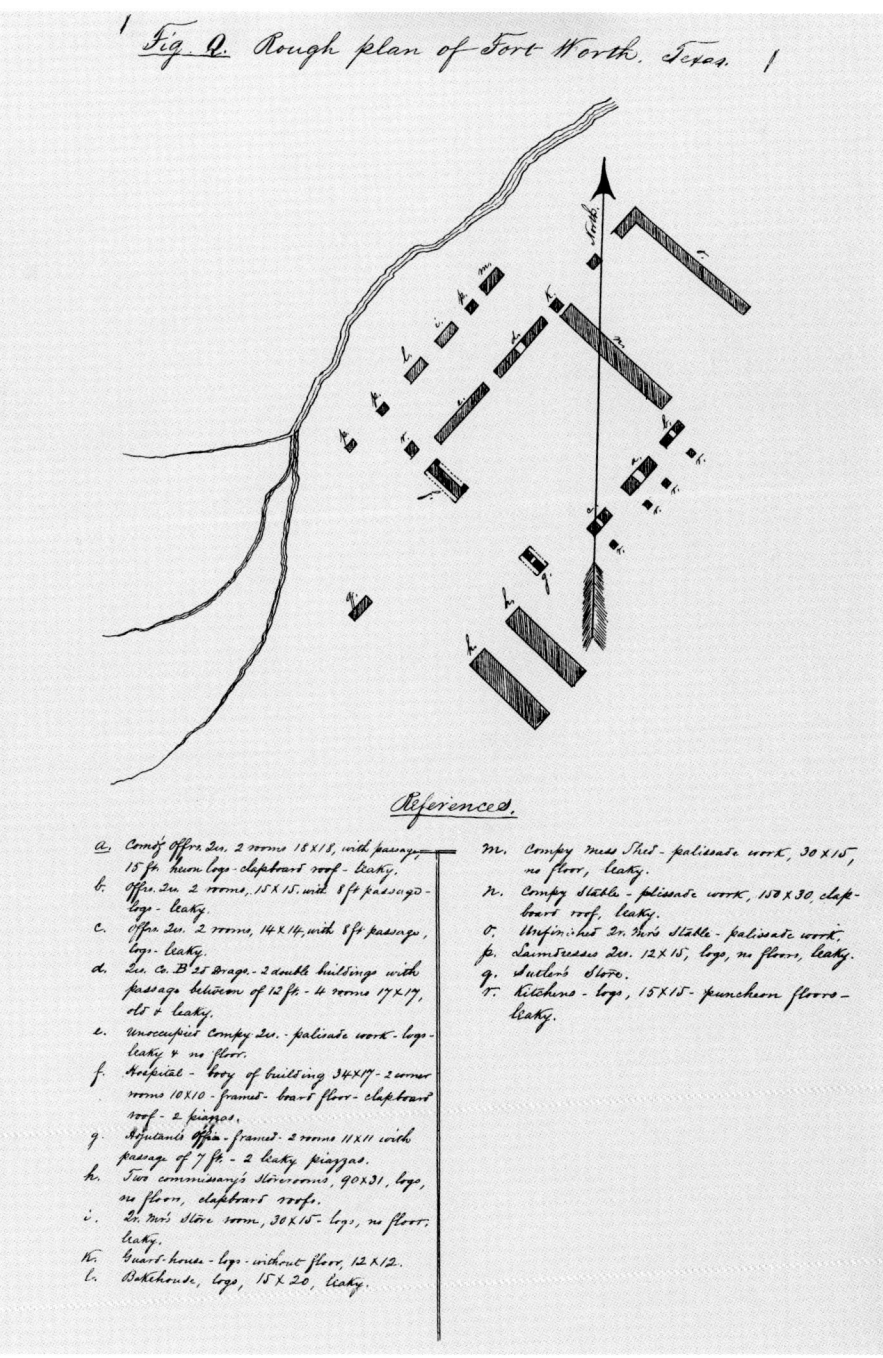

2. The first plan of Fort Worth was laid out in 1849 when Major Ripley Arnold established the post. This plan, showing the commanding officer's quarters, barracks, guard house, and other buildings, was made when Colonel W. G. Freeman inspected the post in September, 1853. Courtesy National Archives, Washington, D. C.

3. Charles Turner was one of the original party that helped locate the site upon which Fort Worth was built in 1849. He later opened a grocery store with E. M. Daggett. Courtesy J. C. Turner, Fort Worth.

4. The sutler at the old fort was Press Farmer, whom Major Arnold found living in a tent on the present site of the Tarrant County courthouse with his wife and baby daughter. As sutler, Farmer performed the usual duties of the quartermaster and the post exchange, selling biscuits, brass-button polish, other soldier goods, and some luxury items like chewing tobacco. He has, therefore, been called the first merchant in Fort Worth. Courtesy *Fort Worth Star-Telegram*.

5. E. M. Daggett, known as "Captain" from his Mexican War days, turned the old army stable into Fort Worth's first hotel. Daggett and his brothers, Henry and C. B., were among the first settlers in Fort Worth. Courtesy *Fort Worth Star-Telegram*.

6. John Peter Smith, called the "Father of Fort Worth" by Captain Paddock. Smith was the first school teacher in Fort Worth. He was in turn a surveyor, lawyer, Texas Ranger, and mayor of Fort Worth. An active promoter of the city, he died in 1901 while in St. Louis on business. Courtesy Mrs. Edward Hudson, Fort Worth.

7. The Fort Worth and Denver City House and the Hutchins Hotel dominate this Fort Worth scene in the mid 1870s. Courtesy Fort Worth Public Library.

8. P. B. Binyon's Transfer Office. Courtesy W. D. Smith, Fort Worth.

9. Boaz and Battle operated this cotton yard on the courthouse square in the 1870s and 1880s. Courtesy *Fort Worth Star-Telegram*.

10. The first stone courthouse in Tarrant County was begun in 1861, but construction was discontinued during the Civil War. K. M. Van Zandt found the uncompleted courthouse representative of the psychological gloom that engulfed Fort Worth immediately after the war. It was completed in the early 1870s but burned in 1876, and was superseded by this building. The structure pictured, built in 1876-1877, is in the bird's eye views of Fort Worth in both 1886 and 1891. It was razed in 1894 to make way for the present courthouse. Courtesy Fort Worth Public Library.

11. This was market day in Fort Worth on the southwest corner of the courthouse square in 1877. Farm wagons have taken every available "parking space." The streets in the background are Weatherford and Houston. Photograph by Crawford & Wheeler. Courtesy Fort Worth Public Library.

12. The Fort Worth public square, near the courthouse, in the 1860s.
Courtesy Witherspoon and Associates, Fort Worth.

13. Located in the 200 block of West Weatherford, H. Dugan's wagon yard reportedly was a gathering place for casual friends and conversations. This photograph was taken about 1880. Courtesy Fort Worth Public Library.

14. This 1880 photograph shows W. G. Turner's place, a grocery and meat market. Like many of the merchants of the day, Turner also sold fresh produce and dry goods. Mr. and Mrs. Turner are pictured, the second and third persons from the left. Courtesy J. C. Turner, Fort Worth.

II. THE BOOM YEARS

15. The oldest son of Isaac Van Zandt, congressman and minister for the Republic of Texas, Khleber M. Van Zandt surveyed for the railroad and practiced law in East Texas before he came to Fort Worth following the Civil War. He was president of the bank of Tidball, Van Zandt, and Company, a firm that later became the Fort Worth National Bank. Courtesy Fort Worth National Bank.

Reconstruction, a difficult burden for most of the South, was instrumental in starting Fort Worth on the road to recovery. Confederate soldiers, returning to their homes, found the conditions of carpetbag rule intolerable. All around them were new restrictions of government, deflated economy and, in most instances, bone-crushing poverty. Many young men headed west to seek whatever degree of independence they could find. Some came to Fort Worth. Among them was a Confederate veteran from East Texas, Major K. M. Van Zandt. He wrote of his arrival:

> Fort Worth, as I first saw it late on an August afternoon in 1865, presented a sad and gloomy picture. The town had been laid out according to the general style, with a square in the center with stores surrounding it. A courthouse had been started in 1860. The rock walls had been built up as high as the first story, and there the work had stopped. The very looks of those walls accentuated the picture of desolation. The deserted officers' quarters were still standing on the northeast side of the square, and the parade ground was still to be seen. On the south and west sides of the square there were a few business houses, some of them stone or brick and two stories high. All of them had the shelves empty and the doors locked.
>
> The town had lost much of its former population due to the war. The young men had nearly all gone into the Confederate Army. Many of them had fallen on the field of battle, and those who had returned home had fallen prey to the apathy of the old men who remained at home and became weary with four long years of watching and waiting. I think there were not over 250 people—counting men, women and children. There were many more houses than there were people to occupy them. The business life of the town consisted of a blacksmith shop owned by the King brothers, a flour mill owned by a Mr. Mock, a shoe cobbler's shop, and possibly one other store of some kind. The town could not boast of a post office. Not even a saloon was here then.

Khleber Miller Van Zandt became the focal point of Fort Worth's greatest economic boom. He was well-equipped for his role.

The Van Zandt family came to America before the Revolution. When K. M. was born in 1836 in Maxwell, Tennessee, his father Isaac was a partner in a mercantile store. The firm failed in the Panic of 1837. K. M.'s father was left with a number of debts. Hoping to utilize his unusual talent for public speaking, he studied for the bar and was admitted to practice. In 1838 he made an exploratory trip to East Texas, and in the following year returned for his family.

Isaac Van Zandt's required period of residency for public office was barely completed at Elysian Fields, Harrison County, before he was elected to the Texas Congress. He quickly became an outstanding member. In 1842, Texas named him *charge d'affaires* to the United States to supervise the delicate maneuvering for statehood. He later became candidate for governor, and was regarded as the front contender when he died unexpectedly of yellow fever during the arduous campaign of 1847.

K. M. Van Zandt attended public schools in Marshall. He later returned to Tennessee for higher education, receiving his diploma at Franklin College, near Nashville. He studied law, and was admitted to the bar in 1858.

Early in 1861, he was enrolled as lieutenant in Bass's Grays, a Marshall military unit preparing for "the call." When it came, the group went with the Seventh Texas into the thickest of the fighting. Van Zandt was captured by Union forces shortly after the Confederate disaster at Fort Donelson, Tennessee, in February of 1862. He was interned at Johnson's Island on Lake Erie. Exchanged in September of that year, he returned to the fighting, and was in the midst of action at Chickamauga and Missionary Ridge. Although Van Zandt escaped injury, exposure and lack of rest resulted in severe lung trouble. Too ill to ride from the battlefield at Missionary Ridge, he was taken to Dalton, Georgia, in a wagon. He later was granted a leave of absence to return to East Texas for recuperation, and to seek recruits. He was there when General Robert E. Lee surrendered.

Because of what he termed "the many carpetbaggers and undesirable characters" who came to East Texas, Van Zandt set out with four friends for West Texas. He once described his trip:

> As we journeyed West, the distance between the villages grew greater, and the way grew lonelier. The enthusiasm of the men with me began to wane. One by one they said, "You are going too far," and they turned back. I rode on alone until I reached Fort Worth, 180 miles from Marshall.

Despite Fort Worth's prevailing aura of gloom, Van Zandt talked with the residents, and "learned enough... to make me realize the possibilities of the place and to decide to cast my lot here and grow with the town." Van Zandt rented a house and moved his wife and four children to Fort Worth. He first started a mercantile store. He was so convinced of the town's future that he gambled an investment of three hundred dollars to buy the block bounded by Main and Houston and Third and Fourth Streets.

Reconstruction was felt in Fort Worth, but not as keenly as in other sections of the South. Approximately half of the freed slaves remained in Tarrant County. Many continued to work for their former owners under altered conditions. Some, for a time, were in worse circumstances economically. There were rumors of thievery by impoverished Negroes. The Ku Klux Klan rode, but briefly. Some farmers between Fort Worth and Cleburne organized to protect their field hands. They prepared a trench and greeted the Klan with a volley from shotguns. That ended local enthusiasm for night-riding.

In an effort to block Yankee domination, a Tarrant County group went to Austin to present a slate of candidates for Reconstruction office. The plan was successful; the county emerged with one of the first governments established in the South after the war.

Fort Worth soon was simply too busy to worry about what some Yankee thought it should be doing. The spark that enlivened Fort Worth's days—and nights—came from cattle, and thousands of them. Fort Worth's major role in the postbellum cattle industry stemmed more from circumstance than planning.

In the fall of 1865, Captain Eph Daggett drove a large herd to Shreveport.[17] The drive was not successful. Negro soldiers in blue lined the roads east of Marshall. Captain Daggett felt that they were more arrogant than necessary. To avoid them, the cattle were driven into the brush. At Shreveport, the market was low, the Longhorns brought only six dollars a head above expenses. Daggett remembered the drive as the most difficult in his career.

With the market to the east virtually closed, more than 200,000 Texas Longhorns were driven northward in 1866 in an effort to run the blockade imposed by Missouri against Texas fever, a tick conveyed disease to which Texas cattle were immune. Most of the traildrivers attempted to go around Missouri by heading through eastern Kansas. But the section was settled mostly by Missouri farmers, who knew firsthand of the dangers of Texas fever to their domestic stock. The drives encountered considerable difficulty; the results were mixed. Enough were successful that in 1867 another batch of Texas cattle went up the trail.

Joseph G. McCoy, a young man who was to have a profound influence on Fort Worth, was hard at work in Kansas in an effort to find a compromise among farmers, railroad officials and merchants to take advantage of the potential wealth in Texas cattle. Most Kansas residents were unreceptive to

McCoy's project. One railroad executive showed McCoy the door (a mistake that eventually made Chicago, not St. Louis, the major meat packing center of the nation). Colorado, Nebraska, Kansas, Missouri, Illinois and Kentucky had enacted strong laws barring the importation of Texas cattle, but in Kansas McCoy had found a loophole. Under certain conditions, stockmen could take Texas cattle to a loading point for shipment out of state, provided they did not drive the cattle within five miles of any settler without his permission in writing.

In Abilene, at midpoint in the 1867 season, McCoy found a marketplace where those conditions might be met. Although some local opposition to his plan existed, he sent a messenger down the trail to inform drivers en route northward that they would find a market for their cattle in Abilene. When Texas cowboys trailed in, sold their cattle, and started hunting such luxuries as butter, eggs, potatoes, and garden delicacies, and grain and hay for their horses, all opposition to Texas cattle collapsed. That fall, McCoy sent circulars to all points in Texas, advising traildrivers of the new market. Returning cowboys helped to spread the word.

In July of that year, William (Buffalo Bill) Mathewson returned to Fort Arbuckle[18] with two white youths he had rescued from the Comanches. At the fort he met a Texas traildriver who asked his advice on the best way to travel to Kansas with a herd of cattle. Mathewson suggested "Chisholm's trail." By the following spring, a new term had entered the language, and Chisholm became a profound influence on Fort Worth's fortunes after his own death.

Jesse Chisholm, of Scotch and Cherokee ancestry, was born in Tennessee in 1805 or 1806. He came west with the early Cherokee migrations to the new tribal lands on the Arkansas River. He married a Creek woman, and from 1832 until his death he operated various trading posts in the Indian Nations. By trial and error, Chisholm eventually found the best north-south route, utilizing available water and good crossings. He often was employed as a guide, and "Chisholm's trail" became fairly well-known. He died on March 4, 1868, in the spring that brought thousands of Longhorns up his trail. His death was attributed to cholera, caused by eating bear's grease poisoned by being melted in a brass kettle.

Fortunately for Fort Worth, his trail was almost straight north.[19]

The town did not make much of an impression on the early traildrivers. M. A. Withers of Lockhart came through early in the spring of 1868 with 600 big steers. "Only one or two stores were there then," he said. W. R. Massengale, who went up the trail in 1870, recalled: "We took the New Chisum (sic) Trail, went by the way of Fort Worth, which was a small village of one or two small business houses, a blacksmith shop and I think a school house and about twenty families. The Indians were bad in that section and we had a double watch on every night which made it hard for us." George W. Saunders, who made his first trail drive at the age of 17 in 1871, wrote: "Between (Cleburne and Fort Worth) the country was somewhat level and untimbered, and was full of prairie chickens and deer. When we reached Fort Worth we crossed the Trinity River under the bluff . . . . Fort Worth was then but a very small place, consisting of only a few stores."

Seventy-five thousand cattle were driven to Abilene during the 1868 season; in 1869 the total was doubled. Fort Worth was the last chance for drovers to buy flour, bacon, beans, dried fruit, coffee, and other necessities for the long drive across the Nations. Fort Worth, the first town that most traildrivers reached in returning from Kansas, also outfitted them for the final leg of the homeward trip.

The cattle industry gave the town its first economic security. The relationships formed between the businessmen and Texas cattlemen in the era of the trail drives eventually were perhaps even more important.

Another source of income came from the Plains. The great American buffalo slaughter was under way, and hides began to arrive in Fort Worth. Wagon freighters often hauled full loads on each round trip, taking supplies to the Plains, and returning with buffalo hides.

The population of Fort Worth doubled between 1865 and 1868. Growth was boosted further in 1871 by rumors of the coming of the railroad.

In July of 1872, Colonel Thomas A. Scott, president of the Texas & Pacific Railroad, a party of Eastern capitalists and Texas Governor J. W. Throckmorton arrived in Fort Worth to study the town's potential as a rail point. Traveling with the group was Colonel John Weiss Forney, editor of the *Philadelphia Press,* who published his observations in a book:[20]

> The town of Fort Worth contains some twelve or fifteen hundred habitants, several churches, good schools, and a large court-house, in the centre of the plaza, constructed of yellowish limestone, resembling Joliet marble. It remains in an unfinished condition. Fort Worth is beautifully situated on a broad plateau. Immediately on its northern and western borders are the waters of the Clear Fork and West Fork Rivers, which here unite and form the Trinity. The banks are steep and precipitous, one hundred and ten feet in height, covered with luxuriant foliage.
>
> The prospect from this plateau is grand beyond description, decidedly the finest we enjoyed during our visit to Texas—especially in the western direction and the course pursued by the Texas and Pacific Railroad. For fifty miles away there lay stretched before us a succession of cultivated fields, interspersed with belts of timber, wide expanses of prairie lands with the natural grass, and in the dim horizon, so far off as

to be barely distinguished from the clouds themselves, a succession of lofty mountains [sic]. The hotel accommodations at Fort Worth need to be greatly enlarged, but there are comfortable private dwellings, and the citizens are kind, courteous, and hospitable. The breezes at this elevation far surpass anything we experienced.

Fort Worth is a city set on a hill, and as the point of junction between two branches of the Texas and Pacific, is particularly enviable, inasmuch as from this locality the Grand Trunk line to the Pacific will be projected and pushed. Lands in the vicinity of Fort Worth have been selling at exceedingly low prices, but they will be greatly enhanced on account of its proposed railroad facilities. During the last year 500,000 head of cattle were driven through Fort Worth on their way to Missouri and Kansas, and as we left the town we met a single drove containing 1,250 head.

Forney's enthusiasm apparently was shared by the visiting capitalists. Colonel Scott, a frank trader, told the town's residents exactly what would be required to bring the railroad to Fort Worth: "I want 320 acres of land south of town, running from the West Fork on the east (sic) to the Clear Fork on the west. In consideration of this, I will proceed as rapidly as possible to build the Texas and Pacific Railroad to your town."

Within hours, and on the same day, Major K. M. Van Zandt, Colonel T. J. Jennings, Captain Eph Daggett and Judge H. G. Hendricks pledged the land.

In anticipation of the railroad, Fort Worth's population nearly doubled again in the following year. All things seemed possible. Wholesale grocery stores and lumberyards were opened to take choice locations. Drygoods stores, drugstores, livery stables, a photography studio, and an ice cream parlor were among the many businesses that were launched to serve the future railhead. Lawyers arrived to handle the active trade in real estate. And Fort Worth's first civic-oriented newspaper assumed the dominant part it was to play in Fort Worth's career. Its editor, B. B. Paddock, in effect became the civic conscience.

A former scout for the Confederacy, Paddock arrived in Fort Worth in October of 1872. Although a native of Ohio, he had gone to Mississippi to enlist at the age of 16 upon the outbreak of the Civil War. At 17, he was one of the youngest officers in the Confederate Army, and served with distinction throughout the war. He then studied for the bar, and for a time practiced law. Seeking a more active life, he traveled west, and came to Fort Worth. After studying the town, Paddock went to see merchant K. M. Van Zandt. Both were to reminisce over that interview:

"What would you like to do?" Van Zandt asked.

"I would like to run a newspaper, sir," Paddock said.

"Well, we have one here, and we will give it to you if you will operate it," Van Zandt told him.

Van Zandt, lamenting the lack of a newspaper, in 1871 had organized a company to buy the printing equipment of the defunct *Quitman Herald*. The price was a wagonload of wheat. On the old Washington press acquired in the transaction, the company started publication of the *Fort Worth Democrat*. In its first year, there had been several editors. Paddock eventually became full owner.

Early in 1873, Paddock set the tenor of his editorship with what came to be known as the "Tarantula Map." It depicted Fort Worth as a blob in the center, with the "legs" of future railroads and stage lines leading off in various directions.

Efforts had been made for incorporation and a civic government. Van Zandt, serving as state representative, introduced the charter, written by Judge J. Y. Hogsett, to the Thirteeenth Legislature. The prospect of additional taxes spawned some opposition. Writing in the *Democrat*, Paddock chided some citizens for their views. He said opponents of incorporation were "criminally culpable."

The Legislature enacted the bill on February 15, 1873. The measure became effective March 1. On April 3, Dr. W. P. Burts was elected first mayor. Aldermen were M. B. Loyd, M. D. McCall, A. Blakeney, W. J. Boaz and J. P. Alexander. E. S. Terrell was elected marshal.

A minor fire led Paddock to rant, editorially, over the foolishness of Fort Worth's attempt to exist without proper fire-fighting facilities. Through his efforts, the M. T. Johnson Hook and Ladder Company was organized on May 2, 1873.

With incorporation, new businesses, evidence of construction throughout the town, a good traildriving season, a steady stream of hides from Jacksboro, and the railroad on the way, Fort Worth was a confident, prosperous town in the summer of 1873. The lean times seemed to be over.

Then in September came the Panic of 1873, one of the worst financial setbacks the nation had ever experienced.

The New York Stock Exchange remained closed for ten days. A month later, the effect was felt in the cattle trade. Traildrivers arriving in Kansas late that season found no market. A few leased grasslands, hoping for improved conditions in the spring. Others killed thousands of cattle for the hides and tallow. In late fall, a "killing blizzard" swept through the cattle country. It was the first of several storms that destroyed herds far into Texas that winter.

Railroad construction was halted throughout the nation. Thirty miles from Fort Worth, at Eagle Ford, the Texas & Pacific stopped laying track.

The effect on Fort Worth was disastrous. Paddock later described the scene:

> Professional men from all over the country who had left comfortable homes and good businesses to come here and begin their fortunes anew, faced inevitable ruin. The population dwindled as rapidly as it had grown. Stores and dwellings were vacated by the score. Business was at a standstill and gloom and despondency was everywhere visible. The road to the eastward was filled with people who were leaving the town in as large numbers as a few days previously they had sought it.
>
> Eagle Ford which had sprung into a town of more than a thousand was as quickly depopulated — the people for the most part moving back to Dallas. It was the opportunity for that city. Had the Panic broken thirty days later so that it would have been practicable to have completed the road to Fort Worth before suspending operations, Dallas would have been a good county seat town instead of a thriving city . . .
>
> The decimation of Fort Worth left here about one thousand people. Many of them stayed because they could not well get away. Others remained because their faith in the ultimate growth and preeminence of the city was not shaken by this disaster . . .
>
> The grass literally grew in the streets. This was not a metaphor to indicate stagnation, but a doleful fact.

Dallas, with a railroad, was in a better position to see the humor in Fort Worth's situation. The *Dallas Herald* published an article by a former Fort Worth lawyer, Robert E. Cowart, who wrote that Fort Worth was such a drowsy place that he saw a panther sleep in the street by the courthouse.[21]

Paddock noted that Cowart had "a keen sense of the ridiculous and verbiage that can make an Indian's hair curl." But he added that the story was an accurate assessment of conditions. "No attempt was made to deny or explain the charge," he wrote. "It was accepted as fact."

Fort Worth's newly elected city officials agreed to serve the impoverished government without pay. As the second election neared the following spring, Editor Paddock found little interest among voters:

> On the twelfth of next month the regular election for officers will take place. At present there seems to be but little necessity for a city government, [but] we think it unwise to let the election go by default, as some suggest.

Even in the midst of a nation in the grips of a severe depression, Fort Worth's plight was given widespread notice. Major K. M. Van Zandt received an offer of a partnership in a Houston bank from friends who apparently thought him desperate. He declined, suggesting that they come to Fort Worth and go into business with him. The Houston bankers complimented Van Zandt on his obviously unshakable faith in Fort Worth.

Van Zandt backed that faith with money. Thomas A. Tidball and John Wilson had opened a private bank early in 1873. After the Panic, Wilson decided to return to Missouri. Van Zandt, J. J. Jarvis, John Peter Smith and Tidball subscribed $7,500 each for a $30,000 capital stock, and reopened the private bank under the name of Tidball, Van Zandt and Company.

The remaining merchants met to discuss Fort Worth's precarious situation. "It was apparent that if Fort Worth was to become a city something had to be done very soon," Van Zandt explained.

A plan was devised and the town was plunged into the most dramatic concerted effort in its history.

Major Van Zandt and four other civic leaders went to Marshall to talk with Frank S. Bond, vice president of Texas & Pacific Railroad. Van Zandt maneuvered Bond into a statement to the effect that rails were not the problem. The railroad could buy rails on credit. "But we have no money to pay for grading the road," Bond said.

"Well, we will take the contract for grading the road and accept your note due in a reasonable length of time," Van Zandt told him.

At first, Bond thought the offer was a joke. Once convinced that his visitors were serious, Bond agreed to come to Fort Worth to discuss the proposal further.

When he arrived, the Tarrant County Construction Company had been organized with a subscribed capital stock of $25,000. Bond agreed to the plan. The Tarrant County company began work, grading the bed for the rail line to Fort Worth.

Neighboring towns regarded Fort Worth's new bootstrap effort with amusement. The *Dallas Herald* and the *Sherman Register* were especially outspoken. The *Register* commented: "the probability is that their scheme will terminate just as many a one before, and exhaust itself ere they commence work." Paddock replied:

> The *Register* never made a greater mistake. The people of Fort Worth heretofore have held town meetings and made buncombe speeches, and it all has ended with "resolved." But this time they have put their hands deep down into their purses and have gone to work with a vim and energy worthy of the importance of the work at hand, and they will not abate their vigor until the road bed is completed from Eagle Ford to Fort Worth.

The railroad's failure to complete the construction by January of 1874 had resulted in forfeiture of the land donated for the depot and sidings. This gift was renewed on October 23, 1875—on the condition that the railroad would be completed within two years of the date.

Fort Worth's enthusiasm grew steadily. On November 6, 1875, the *Democrat* observed:

> The news having gone abroad of the organization of the Tarrant County Construction Company and their determination to resume work on the T&P, between this [sic] and Eagle Ford, has already produced a good effect on the business of our town. It has infused a new life and vigor into our people which reacts on those coming here with good results. Vacant houses are filling up; hotels are crowded; stages and hacks come in loaded, and everything is beginning to assume the appearance of life, activity and enterprise, which was shown here in the early days of 1873.

A minor tragedy failed to dampen Fort Worth's mood. It occurred on March 29, 1876. The *Democrat* reported:

BLAZES!

– – –

Court House Burned!

– – –

TOTAL DESTRUCTION OF
THE COUNTY RECORDS!

– – –

LOSS INCALCULABLE!

> Wednesday morning between four and five o'clock, the Court House was discovered to be on fire and burning rapidly. Mr. Joel Hancock, constable of Precinct No. 8 and J. W. Roy, constable of Precinct No. 2 and another person were sleeping in the office of Chief Justice (J. S.) Morris' in the southwest upper corner of the building, and were the first to discover the fire and give the alarm. The city was soon aroused and the Hook and Ladder Company and citizens were soon on the ground; but the fire had made such headway that it was impossible to check its progress.

The *Democrat* reported that the origin of the blaze was not known, but that evidence indicated that it had started in the office of the Clerk of the District Court. The account added that while the county's records of deeds might in time be restored from the files of abstract offices, there was no way to make compensation for the parties who had cases in litigation in court, as all papers and minutes were "totally destroyed." Paddock observed:

> Had the records of the courts been saved, the loss would have been slight, as the better workmanship and modern improvements that can be utilized in rebuilding the house would compensate for the loss

incurred . . . . If it should transpire that the fire was the work of an incendiary, as it is believed by many, we hope the fiend may be discovered and punished.

A few days later the *Democrat* reported:

Since the destruction of the Court House we have made diligent inquiry among the citizens of all portions of the county and find them very much united in favor of building another Court House as speedily as possible. The style and size of the building creates some diversity of opinion, though all agree that it should be such an one as would be an ornament, and do credit to our county.

Work on the railroad continued at a faster pace. On July 6 the *Democrat* observed:

We know of no term that expresses more fully the condition of affairs in Fort Worth at the present time than "red hot." In every line of business there is great activity which increases day by day as the time when the steam whistle shall wake the echos [sic] in our city approaches. The population of the city may be said to be hourly increasing, so rapid is the influx of people who come to locate.

Then a new complication arose. The State's land grant agreement with the railroad was to be voided if the railroad did not reach Fort Worth before adjournment of that session of the Legislature.

Word came that the Legislature was about to adjourn without granting an extension.

News also came that Tarrant County's representative, Nicholas H. Darnell, was seriously ill, unable to leave his bed.

Fort Worth refused to admit defeat.

On each of the next 15 days of the Legislature, Darnell was carried on a cot into the House chambers to cast his vote to block adjournment.

During those 15 days, the residents of Fort Worth worked around the clock to bring the railroad the last few miles. Volunteers went out to assist in any way they could. Business firms closed their doors and sent their employees out to work on the railroad. Fort Worth women worked in shifts, preparing food and refreshments. Texas & Pacific threw all its resources into the effort.

When the tracks reached Sycamore Creek east of town, there was no time to worry about a proper trestle. Lumber and ties were stacked to span the creek. From there on, no pretense was made of building a roadbed. "Ties were laid on the ground supported at either end by stones picked up from the right of way and the rails spiked to them," Paddock wrote. "It was as crooked as the proverbial ram's horn, but it bore up the rails."

The *Dallas Herald* grudgingly admitted that it might have been wrong in aiming so much derision at Fort Worth's efforts for a railroad. Paddock did not allow the opportunity to pass for a reply. He wrote: "An honest confession is said to be good for the soul; and if the *Herald,* and the City of Dallas in general has [sic] any soul, we hope this confession, and others they will yet be compelled to make, will prove beneficial and efficacious . . . Retributive justice will yet overtake many others besides the *Herald.* We have never had much confidence in deathbed repentance."

On July 12 the *Democrat* reported:

> There is a continual and incessant stream of buggies, carriages, hacks and persons on horseback going to and from Sycamore Creek, who gather there every day to witness the throngs of men, who are at work like bees on the bridging and piling on the bottom. On Sunday there were hundreds of spectators on the grounds all day. Some of them came long distances, and many had never seen a railroad or anything pertaining to one, and were much interested and highly entertained by the sight of the engines and the busy workers.

The great day arrived. On July 18, Paddock made a personal appeal:

> This evening at four o'clock the construction train will cross the last boundary line of the town, and it is suggested that Fort Worth, men, women and children, old and young be present and give them a rousing welcome. Let every one bring a basket with boiled hams, light bread, cold chicken, salads, pickles, wines, anything, everything that is good, and give the hard handed strong armed men who have been at work night and day, a rousing welcome. Let there be no standing back.

At 11:23 a.m. on July 19, 1876, the first train arrived in Fort Worth. The occasion set off one of Fort Worth's most memorable celebrations. Some of the speakers were so carried away by the excitement that they made predictions that Fort Worth some day would have a population of five thousand or more.

Civic pride flared. A contractor who had planned to pay off his men in Dallas was informed that Fort Worth residents would consider it an act of heresy. Mayor G. H. Day pledged that if the men were paid off in Fort Worth, none would be arrested for drunkenness. The men were paid off in Fort Worth.

The long-awaited economic boom quickly materialized. So swift was Fort Worth's growth that by the first of the following year, an estimated 1,000 persons lived in tents in and around the city limits.

After the economic disaster and hard winter of 1873, the cattle trade had steadily regained ground. The first herd of the 1876 season arrived in Fort Worth April 7, and by "Railroad Day" thousands of cattle were outfitted for the trail, including five herds totaling 12,000 belonging to Major Seth Mabry. "The trail is swarming with cattle," the *Democrat* reported. By the end of the season, the *Democrat* had logged 204,438 head. Another 60,000 were grazing near Fort Worth, awaiting shipment over the new railroad.

The buffalo slaughter out beyond Fort Griffin was at its peak; at one time 60,000 hides were piled on a platform near the railroad, awaiting shipment. During the season, 200,000 hides were transported through Fort Worth. The hunters received about one dollar for each hide.

The *Dallas Herald's* sport with the panther story was not forgotten. "Everyone named everything 'Panther,'" Paddock wrote. "There were panther stores, panther meat markets, panther saloons."

The *Fort Worth Democrat* added to its masthead a drawing of a panther *couchant* beside a railroad track which passed through a thriving town. At the bottom of the emblem, wording proclaimed: *Where The Panther Laid* [sic] *Down*.

Two live panther cubs were found and housed in a handsome cage at the fire hall. Several saloons adopted live panther mascots. The practice had its hazards. On at least one occasion a saloon patron was severely mauled.

The *Dallas Herald* took the sarcastic use that Fort Worth made of its joke in good grace. The newspaper suggested that if Fort Worth would provide excursion rates, a thousand or more Dallas County residents might ride over on the train to see where the panther once slept. The excursion train was not needed. Fort Worth was determined that Dallas would not soon forget the matter. During the next several years Fort Worth's contribution to each Dallas parade or celebration included the two fire hall panthers on a float pulled by four matched white horses and escorted by 40 "Panther City" citizens in white uniforms.

For the residents of Fort Worth, the railroad was the realization of a dream. Editor M. M. Brannan of the *Fort Worth Standard* assured them the dream had not ended when he wrote on October 11, 1876:

> The depot is still there, and so are the many trains which are loading with cotton, wheat, and all kinds of produce, which seek Fort Worth as an outlet to the great marts of the continent.

A few weeks later, Brannan offered further reassurance:

> In company with Mr. Howard Peak, we drove down to the depot and observed with astonishment the amount of business done there. Thousands upon thousands of feet of lumber, innumerable bales of cotton awaiting shipment, box goods, heavy groceries, bagging and ties, and every article of merchandise in crowded profusion.

The railroad and resulting business boom provided confidence for the start of a new Courthouse. On November 3, 1876, the *Standard* reported:

> The old Courthouse has been torn down and a great pile of "gray sad rocks" is all that remains of the grim old ruins from this whilom temple of justice . . . . The foundation of the new Courthouse has been commenced and soon a new and splendid edifice will have supplanted the old eyesore now happily gone forever.

With the increased population, Editor Paddock of the *Democrat* hounded Fort Worth on the theme that the time had come to assume more of the status of a city. He cited certain shortcomings. "There are so many loose stones in the streets that the progress of vehicles is greatly impeded," he wrote. He added: "No city in northern Texas can boast [of] such a limited supply of good sidewalks." He suggested that the city could at least build a sidewalk down either Houston or Main Street to serve the new depot.

The town made valiant efforts to rise to the civic status that Paddock advocated. By late December of 1876, streetcars were serving the length of Main Street, and by March of 1877, the downtown streets blossomed with gas lamps.

The streetcars furnished entertainment as well as transportation. The two small cars made continuous round trips from the Courthouse to the T&P station. Passengers were provided with a single wooden seat running along each side of the car. Power was furnished by what Paddock described as "one mule something larger than a West Texas jack rabbit." Often the cars jumped the tracks, sometimes at mud puddles, and the passengers were called upon to dismount and to lift the car back onto the tracks. Some passengers said they worked harder than the mule. The drivers were known to offer free rides to ensure sufficient manpower aboard. Runaway mule cars provided occasional diversion. In at least one recorded instance, a driver stopped at a saloon for a drink, and the mule set out for the Trinity River, taking the car with him. During the first year of operation, the two cars made 160 trips per day, carrying an average of 440 passengers for a $22 profit.

Although Fort Worth businessmen were jubilant over the return of good times, Paddock insisted that the boom should be even better. He pointed out that some traildrivers had mapped out a new route to Kansas a hundred miles or so to the west, passing Fort Griffin to cross the Red River at Doan's Store. During the first two years this "Western Trail" was used, Fort Worth hardly noticed the effect. But in 1878 Editor Paddock chided Fort Worth merchants for allowing Fort Griffin to attract 150,000 cattle that season. "Had our businessmen been equally active in securing this immense drive, the season total (here) would not have fallen short of 200,000," he wrote. "Experience is a dear teacher. We hope that their eyes will be opened to their best interests next year."

Paddock apparently made his point. In 1879 merchants sent a spokesman, Dave Blair, down the trail to sell traildrivers on Fort Worth's advantages as a supply center. The effort paid off. Fort Worth's total that year was 135,000, and Fort Griffin's 101,010. The rivalry was replete with barbed exchanges between the *Fort Worth Democrat* and the *Fort Griffin Echo,* leading to taunts for a wager. No agreement on terms was reached.

Although Fort Worth and Fort Griffin were rivals for the cattle, they remained partners in the buffalo harvest. Fort Griffin, called the World's Buffalo Capital, freighted hides and bones to Fort Worth for rail shipment. At one time, hides were stacked ten to fifteen feet high over a ten-acre tract on the T&P Reservation, awaiting shipment.

Editor Paddock's Tarantula Map became less visionary as more and more of the "legs" were realized. Stage lines provided regular service to Fort Concho (San Angelo), Weatherford, Jacksboro, Fort Belknap, Fort Griffin, Cleburne, and Decatur. In 1878, Fort Worth became the easternmost point of the world's longest stage line—a 1,560-mile route to Yuma, Arizona. The trip required seventeen bone-jarring days when the route opened. Greater speed was urged. Editor Paddock explained:

> The cayotes [sic] that inhabited most of the country beyond the Concho could not afford to wait that long for their mail and so the Second Assistant Postmaster General, at the earnest solicitation of the inhabitants, and the contractors, agreed to increase the compensation one hundred per cent if the trip could be made in thirteen days—which was easy . . . . The mail left Fort Worth in a Concord coach pulled by six horses and ran to Tharp Springs [sic], where it was transferred to a surrey with two horses. These went as far as Brownwood, where a buckboard and two bronchos took it the remainder of the way, if they were not interrupted.

Fort Worth was serving as the railhead and passenger center for West Texas. Livery stables and wagon yards occupied much of the town. To accommodate the many travelers, two excellent hotels were opened—the 95-room Mansion in 1876, and the El Paso in 1878. There also were the Transcontinental, the Virginia House, Peers House, the Pacific and the Clark House. In 1876 the Peers House boasted an innovation—"female waiters." The *Fort Worth Standard* observed that they not only were ornamental but also were "exceedingly useful."

On January 16, 1877, Martin B. Loyd incorporated the First National Bank, after selling his interest in "The California and Texas Bank of Loyd, Marklee and Company," which was a lineal descendant of Fort Worth's first bank, Loyd's Exchange Office, established in 1870.[22]

The bank's growth in the first year indicates the strength of the town's economy. After opening in April with $72,000 in deposits, the First National reported $220,000 by year's end, and declared a dividend of 12 per cent.

Fort Worth's second railroad, the Missouri-Kansas-Texas, arrived in May of 1880. Eighteen months later the Santa Fe reached Fort Worth, chiefly through the efforts of Van Zandt and Paddock. Van Zandt obtained a commitment that the railroad would be built into Fort Worth if the town could raise $75,000 toward expenses. A story persisted locally that Van Zandt and Paddock called a meeting of civic leaders, locked the doors, and refused to allow anyone to leave until the total had been pledged.

The 1880 census revealed Fort Worth's population at 6,663. With railroads, stage lines, and banks and merchants attracting clientele throughout West Texas, Fort Worth was well on the way to becoming the city envisioned by Van Zandt, Paddock and other civic leaders who had remained steadfast through her darkest days.

NOTES, THE BOOM YEARS

17. The impression apparently persists, at least in Hollywood circles, that Texas trail driving did not begin until after the Civil War. The truth is that hundreds of thousands of Texas cattle went up the Shawnee Trail into Missouri long before the war, beginning about 1846. Some were trailed to Chicago and St. Louis, and a few to New York City. But Northern cattle were susceptible to "Texas fever," a disease transmitted by ticks. The Texas Longhorns were immune. Missouri farmers began turning back Texas cattle as early as 1853. In 1858 and 1859, a widespread outbreak of fever brought quarantines that effectively closed the Shawnee Trail to Texas cattle and Dallas, on the Shawnee Trail, missed the opportunity to become "Cowtown."

18. Fort Arbuckle was established by Captain Randolph B. Marcy in 1851, on Wild Horse Creek near the present town of Davis, Oklahoma.

19. Historians are in disagreement as to the Chisholm Trail's exact route throughout its length. Seasonal and local conditions, along with crowded situations on the trail, spawned some alternate routes. But historians agree that for the most part today's U.S. 81 closely follows Chisholm's trail across Oklahoma.

20. Colonel John Weiss Forney's book, *What I Saw in Texas,* was published in 1872 by Ringwald & Brown in Philadelphia.

21. This is the favored version of the "Panther City" nickname among 19th century residents, and the one given by Paddock. References to the *Dallas Herald* joke were made weekly in the *Fort Worth Democrat* in the early summer of 1876, as the two papers waged a war of caustic wit. Oliver Knight lists three other versions of the origin of the nickname in his book, *Fort Worth: Outpost on the Trinity.* Two attribute the nickname to actual visits by panthers. The other concerns the difficulty of drunks in making their way home, with their all-fours tracks being mistaken for those of a panther.

22. Captain Martin B. Loyd is mentioned in an 1868 letter as being in Fort Worth, but the exact date he first opened "The Exchange Office of M. B. Loyd" is uncertain. The "traditional date" is 1870. The first indication of his banking activity that survives is a note due in March of 1872.

16. Texas and Pacific Railway Company, train No. 2, somewhere on the track between Marshall and Fort Worth in 1893. Overcoming seemingly impossible obstacles, the railroad had arrived in Fort Worth in the summer of 1876. Amon Carter Museum Collection.

17. View looking south down Main Street in 1880 before the Texas and Pacific Railroad Station was completed. Courtesy W. D. Smith, Fort Worth.

18. Fort Worth's first fire station.
Courtesy Fort Worth Museum of Science and History.

19. Wood, Dickson Mercantile Company. Courtesy *Fort Worth Star-Telegram*.

20. The artist Frederic Remington stayed at the Ellis Hotel, located at the corner of Throckmorton and Third streets in 1888, just three years after its completion. The hotel burned in 1891. Courtesy Fort Worth Public Library.

21. Office of W. B. King, president of the Fort Worth & Rio Grande Railroad, organized and promoted by Captain B. B. Paddock. Courtesy Fort Worth Public Library.

22. The 1898 funeral of Fort Worth merchant David Linsky attracted this crowd of horse-drawn buggies at an early cemetery. Courtesy *Fort Worth Star-Telegram*.

23. J. Y. Hogsett, attorney and author of the city charter, in his Powell Building office. Courtesy Sam B. Cantey III, Fort Worth.

24. Residence of J. Y. Hogsett, Fort Worth. Courtesy Sam B. Cantey III, Fort Worth.

25. The Stag Saloon at the corner of Sixth and Main was one of the favorite afternoon stops for many Fort Worth males. W. A. Hornbeak, proprietor, and Tony Porter entertained the crowds in 1912. Courtesy Fort Worth Public Library.

26. The clothing store of Washer Brothers was one of the earliest department stores in Fort Worth in 1886. Courtesy Witherspoon & Associates, Fort Worth.

27. An early picture of a number of Fort Worth citizens gathered in front of the Fort Worth National Bank. Courtesy Fort Worth National Bank.

28. Market was a daily gathering place in turn-of-the-century Fort Worth. In the background is the old Post Office building at Jennings and Texas. Amon Carter Museum Collection.

29. Quanah Parker and Samuel Burk Burnett. Quanah often visited Fort Worth to confer with the ranchers regarding the rental of Indian land in Indian Territory for grazing cattle. In turn, the ranchers visited Quanah in Indian Territory. Courtesy Benjamin Tahmahkera, Indiahoma, Oklahoma.

30. One of the popular pastimes of earlier days was hemming linen napkins. Left to right: Ida Beall, Mattie Burzon, Mary Malone, Sue Terrell (from Lynchburg, Virginia), Sue Terrell (from Fort Worth), and Virgile Pitner. Courtesy Mrs. Edward Hudson, Fort Worth.

31. The skyline of Fort Worth is in the background in this photograph, taken in the 1880s. Pictured near the fence are Mrs. H. H. Campbell of Matador, Texas, and her son, Harry. Courtesy Norman Bradford, Fort Worth.

III. A BUNCH OF WILDNESS

32. T. I. "Long Hair Jim" Courtright, Fort Worth marshal from 1876 until 1879. He was killed in a well-known gunfight with Luke Short in 1887. Courtesy Fort Worth Public Library.

In 1876, Fort Worth came to grips with a delicate problem. The cowboys, freighters, buffalo hunters, and railroad men who frequented the town's saloons often became rowdy. The visitors usually were in search of entertainment; they preferred questionable diversions, notably gambling and available women. Merchants observed with concern an uncomfortable fact: efforts to curb these pursuits also curtailed business.

The problem had developed over a three-year span. During the first few weeks after the incorporation of Fort Worth in 1873, the City Council passed a series of ordinances against gambling, prostitution, and the wearing of guns. Thus inhibited, visitors did not spend money as they had in the past. Some went elsewhere for their periodic celebrations. The ordinances were suspended, and Fort Worth became known as a tolerant town. Professional gamblers and prostitutes arrived. A section known as Hell's Half Acre grew up around the intersection of Twelfth and Rusk Streets.[23] By 1876, the town was "wide open." Bars, dance halls, sporting houses, shooting galleries, and other forms of entertainment persisted around the clock.

Yet, most of Fort Worth was as uneasy with the wild life as the Theater Comique's piano player, who never knew when the revelers in the balcony might renew the popular competition in shooting the keys off the piano. Drunken freighters, buffalo hunters or cowboys, mistaking directions in the darkness, often attempted to enter private homes. Respectable women were insulted on the street. The ritual of "shooting up the town"—racing the length of the streets, emptying pistols—eventually frayed the strongest nerves.

Clearly, the town needed an imposing figure to keep the peace, yet one whose presence would not necessarily put a damper on uninhibited souls.

The town's answer to this delicate problem was the 1876 election of Marshal Timothy Isaiah "Long Hair Jim" Courtright, who was to have a long, stormy career as Fort Worth's most famous gunman. Not only did "Long Hair Jim" look the part; he also had impressive credentials.

He was a native of Illinois, where — it was said — the family was well acquainted with a young Springfield lawyer, Abraham Lincoln. Barely 17 at the outbreak of the Civil War, Courtright joined the 7th Iowa Infantry and went into battle as a drummer boy. In his first fight, at Belmont, he abandoned the drum for a rifle. There were reports that during the battle he saved the life of General John Alexander Logan. Courtright served as a personal scout for Logan throughout the war, and won high praise at Fort Donelson and Vicksburg. He was wounded three times.

After the war, he signed on as an Army scout for the Indian Wars in the West. Among his companions was James Butler "Wild Bill" Hickock. Leaving the Army about 1870, Courtright married an Arkansas girl, Sarah Elizabeth Weeks, who was a crack shot. For a time the young couple toured with a Wild West show, performing a shooting act. They eventually came to Fort Worth to farm.[24] They later were invited to tour with Buffalo Bill Cody's Wild West, and "Betty Courtright" and "Jim Courtright" shared the billing with Annie Oakley, Lillian Smith and John C. Morgan. In Virginia City, Courtright was wounded by a chunk of wadding from a blank cartridge. He remained in the hospital when the show left town. The couple returned to Fort Worth. Betty Courtright for a time operated a shooting gallery in the 300 block of Main. Courtright was active in the M. T. Johnson Hook and Ladder Company, and the couple became popular in Fort Worth. "You can't but help liking Jim Courtright," a Texas Ranger once said of him.

Courtright loved to gamble, and spent much of his time in the saloons. Well over six feet tall, with shoulder-length hair and fringed buckskins, he was known as one of the fastest gunmen in the West. Some said *the* fastest. He habitually wore two pistols with the butts forward, not for a cross-body draw, but for a single-gun, right-hand pull. In relaxed moments, he often stuck both pistols into a colorful Mexican sash at his waist.

Fort Worth's high esteem for Courtright was reflected in his election as marshal; he polled more than twice the votes of his nearest rival. The Courtrights moved downtown after his election, occupying a house on Calhoun between First and Weatherford.

But Courtright soon learned, much to his regret, that his mission was not to "clean up" Fort Worth. His orders were simply to keep the peace, to adhere to the fine line between inhibiting the big spenders and allowing complete anarchy.

Fort Worth offered all a thirsty man could want in the way of "trail's end" recreation. Some of the saloons became well known throughout the cattle country: Waco Tap; The Headlight Bar; Tivoli Saloon; The Occidental; Our

Friends; The Red Light; Our Comrades; The Beer Garden; Bon Ton; The Cattle Exchange; Horse Head; The White Elephant; Trinity.

The clientele and services varied. Herman Kussatz' Tivoli Saloon was replete with free lunches, German musicians, and some of the best variety shows on the road. Others offered prize fights, dog fights, and cock fights. Faro, keno and poker were the chief attractions of some. At the Theater Comique, Madame Centz' Female Minstrels offered that Paris sensation, the can-can.

The most popular saloon—or at least the most lawless—was the Red Light,[25] a combined bar and dance hall that thoughtfully also furnished the girls. A "rustler" paired off the couples and called the dances. Approximately 20 small rooms were available off the main 30 x 50-foot dance hall. These cribs were supplemented by many shacks in Hell's Half Acre. Others were scattered throughout the town.

Marshal Courtright's emotions apparently were mixed. A gambler, and a friend of gamblers, he clearly had his own ideas on law enforcement. All during his time in office he chafed under various and often contradictory instructions from many quarters on how he should do his job. Most merchants felt he should keep blood from flowing but not the liquor. He was urged not to arrest drunks until they had spent all their money. Some seemed to believe Courtright exceeded his instructions. City officials often sent him into the surrounding area to track down robbers and desperados. Courtright thought that these were wild goose chases designed to get him out of town on busy nights. Courtright was aided in his duties by two night patrolmen, and by two day men, but without the marshal's imposing presence, the deputies often endured beatings.

Fort Worth's lawlessness grew as Hell's Half Acre became a haven for robbers and bandits. Some operated on the Weatherford road in the Trinity bottoms, within pistol shot of the business district. On January 29, 1878, the mail stage to Weatherford was stopped and robbed at the Mary's Creek crossing a few miles west of Fort Worth. Five passengers lost two gold watches and several hundred dollars. On the following day, the T&P mail and express train was stopped at Eagle Ford and robbed by four masked men packing shotguns. Another T&P express train en route to Fort Worth, was halted at Mesquite on April 5, 1878, and robbed.

Some of the holdups were blamed on Sam Bass and his gang, who were believed to be spending some of their time in Hell's Half Acre. Perhaps the *Standard* had Sam Bass in mind in publishing a warning: "There is a class of beings infesting the city needing the closest surveillance."

As Fort Worth's reputation grew, the long-suffering reform forces began to gain strength. In the spring of 1878, Attorney R. E. Beckham announced as a candidate for mayor, heading a "clean-up" council slate. Beckham opened his heated campaign with personal verbal attacks on incumbent Mayor G. H. Day. He promised to put the city's tax structure on an even keel. He pledged to do something about the numerous hogs that ran free in the business district, filling the air with the stench of their wallows. He advocated a law to ban the troublesome street salesmen, who blocked traffic hawking their goods. And, most importantly, he pledged to regulate gambling and prostitution with tougher laws and strict enforcement.

The campaign was bitter, but Beckham and his reform slate won the election.

The new council immediately encouraged Marshal Courtright to enforce the existing laws. For a time, he kept the jail at Second and Rusk well occupied. On Saturday nights, the lockup averaged 25 or more guests.

Word of the crackdown spread throughout the cattle country. The effect was soon noticed.

On April 18, 1879, an advertisement "paid for by many citizens and businessmen" appeared in the *Fort Worth Democrat:*

> The cattle season beginning, we think more freedom ought to be allowed as everyone is aware of the amount of money spent in this city by the cattlemen and cowboys, thus making every trade and business prosper. We notice especially this year that, contrary to their usual custom, almost all of them remain in their camps a few miles from the city and give as the cause the too stringent enforcement of the law closing all places of amusement that attract them.

Mayor Beckham was successful in many of his reform efforts, such as the curbing of hogs and street salesmen. But on the point of law enforcement in Hell's Half Acre, the council again yielded to civic pressure, much to the disgust of Marshal Courtright. The *Democrat* reported that "the dance halls are in full blast again." Trail herds were courted. When Baylis John Fletcher came through Fort Worth on May 7, 1879, with a herd of 2,525 cattle, the hands were divided into shifts so that each could spend some time in town. Fletcher recalled: "Solicitors from the big grocery stores of Fort Worth met us on horseback several miles from the city, bringing such gifts as bottles of whiskey and boxes of fine cigars."

Marshal Courtright resigned, and left town for a while. He accepted an offer to "clean up" Lake Valley, a mining town in New Mexico Territory.

The *Dallas Herald* later asked questions:

> It would be intelligence to the public to know if there are candidates for county judge and county attorney in Tarrant County who propose to enforce the gambling law in case of their election. Are they all running

on free gambling, free whiskey and free grass platforms? Or is there a candidate or two otherwise inclined? Now that Jim Courtright has left town abruptly and in disgust at his bad treatment, the timid law-abiding citizens might elect county officers who would enforce the criminal statutes of the state.

Courtright's stay in New Mexico Territory was livelier. Two Lake Valley ore thieves tried out the new marshal in a gunfight. They became the founders of the town's boot hill. Courtright was credited with three other killings while taming Lake Valley. He then went to work for the Sierra Mining Company as a guard. His Civil War patron, General John A. Logan, who had become a U.S. senator, owned interest in a ranch in nearby American Valley. In May of 1883, shortly after Senator Logan visited the area, the bodies of two men identified as Alexander Grossette and Robert Elsing were found. The deceased partners happened to have owned the water rights to Logan's American Valley ranch. Courtright and five companions were indicted for murder.

With the name of a U.S. senator involved, the case made international headlines. Interest was heightened further when Courtright and a co-defendant, Jim McIntire, escaped jail. The details of their feat were sketchy. A newspaper reporter at the scene said the stories of the sheriff's deputies concerning the escape were "incoherent and inconsistent."

Courtright and McIntire hid out for a while in the surrounding hills, drifted back to Texas, and then headed for Fort Worth. Jim McIntire described their reception:

> When it became known that we were in Fort Worth the excitement ran high, but the people were our friends and we were not molested. After staying with our friends a short time, we took up our residence in a thicket just back of the graveyard until the excitement died down, as we were liable to be surprised and captured at any time.

The furor over the New Mexico murders gradually faded. Courtright came out of hiding. He was appointed deputy marshal. He was mentioned frequently as arresting officer in newspaper accounts of minor crimes. He later opened the T. I. Courtright Commercial Detective Agency.

His position as both a law officer and a wanted man posed complications.

On April 24, 1884, the *Dallas Herald* commented:

> It would seem that the pursuit of Jim Courtright by the New Mexico authorities would never cease. Several parties of rangers as well as officials from the Territory have been here at different times, but have always gone back without serving their warrants.... A day or two ago four Rangers met A. W. Woody and told him they were going to Fort Worth to get a bad man. Woody suggested they go to Courtright and get his assistance. "That's the very man we're after," was the reply.

> It will not be surprising to know that Woody informed Courtright of the fact that the Rangers were after him. The four were at once placed under espionage by Courtright's friends while he with Officer Neeley started to Marine Creek for a fishing picnic. The pair had reached the Trinity when they noticed three of the men who were after Courtright riding some distance behind them. The [buggy] horse was stopped and Courtright deliberately loaded his Winchester, held it across his knee, faced the horsemen and waited. The horsemen turned their animals and rode back to the city. The four were watching the saloons and hotels last night, but if they are after Courtright they will have . . . to go away without him. Courtright has always made but one statement in regard to the matter: "If I go back I will be murdered . . . and I prefer to die where my friends are. I will not be arrested alive, that's all." It is said the great inducement for Courtright's arrest is a reward of $2,000.

The extent of Courtright's popularity in Fort Worth was amply demonstrated on Friday, October 17, 1884. Two Texas Rangers and Albuquerque Chief of Police Harry Richmond arrived in town, ostensibly to seek Courtright's help on another case. Courtright was suspicious, and asked a Fort Worth friend to go with him to the Ginnochio Hotel, where he was to view pictures to identify some wanted men. Through a ruse of the visitors, the friend was detained. Courtright went alone. When he looked up from his careful examination of the pictures, he faced three cocked pistols.

He was disarmed and held under guard in the hotel room until early evening. Betty Courtright sensed something of what had happened when he failed to come home on time. She notified his friends. The probability of his arrest was confirmed when a train arrived from Wichita Falls. A passenger brought the news that Courtright's co-defendant, Jim McIntire, was under arrest in Wichita Falls.

As word spread, a crowd quickly formed in front of the Ginnochio. Estimates of the armed mob ranged as high as two thousand. Tarrant County Sheriff Walter Maddox went to the hotel to talk to the visiting officers. "You can't take that man away from here," he said. "That crowd won't let you and I can't control them."

After looking out the front windows, Richmond and the Rangers tended to agree. They demanded that the sheriff do his duty and keep Courtright in jail until train time.

Sheriff Maddox was Courtright's friend. Yet, he felt he had two heavy obligations—that of his office, and that of preventing bloodshed.

A plan was put into effect. While lawyer William Capps diverted the crowd's attention with a speech, Courtright was whisked out the back door to a carriage waiting in the narrow alley. By the time the crowd became aware of the trick, officers and prisoner were far up the street, headed for the county jail. There Courtright was held while the visiting officers kept watch. They refused to relinquish Courtright entirely to Tarrant County custody.

By Sunday morning, the town was quiet enough that Courtright could be escorted to the Merchants Restaurant near Houston and Second for breakfast. He was taken again for the noon meal.

Plans were made to take him to Austin on the 6 p.m. train. At 5 p.m., Courtright again was taken to the restaurant for supper. The room was unusually crowded. Caroline Brown, the waitress, managed to convey to Courtright by hand signals that pistols were secreted under his table. Toward the end of the meal, Courtright dropped his napkin. He asked Sheriff Richmond to pick it up for him.

"Pick it up yourself," Richmond said.

Courtright reached toward the floor. When his hands returned to the table, they were holding two cocked pistols.

Witnesses said that 20 or more pistols were drawn in the room.[26] No shots were fired. Courtright's friends stepped between the officers and the door as Courtright backed out. His horse was waiting outside. As Courtright mounted and dashed to catch his train, he fired his pistols into the air several times to alert the town to clear the way. At Second and Rusk, in front of the fire station, his horse slipped and fell. Courtright was hurt, but apparently not seriously. He caught the Galveston-bound train.

Courtright went to New York by ship, then to Toronto, and eventually to Walla Walla, Washington Territory. His family joined him there. They remained in exile more than a year.

On January 20, 1886, Courtright again returned to Fort Worth. By that time McIntire's trial was over, and McIntire was cleared of all charges. Courtright surrendered in the hope that he would receive the same treatment.

The Dallas News reported that Fort Worth was "agog with excitement." After visiting friends in Fort Worth, Courtright went to New Mexico, and was acquitted on all charges from lack of evidence. He returned to Fort Worth and reopened his detective agency, with McIntire as a partner.

Courtright's popularity in Fort Worth received a serious setback later that year with a gunfight at Buttermilk Junction. Courtright's conduct was not questioned. Most Fort Worth residents simply felt he was allied with the wrong faction.

Railroad strikes had erupted throughout the nation. The Knights of Labor had begun agitation in Texas as early as 1882, centering attention on Jay Gould and the Wabash Railway Company. The principal issue was pay. The Wabash did not run into Fort Worth; however, by 1886 the Knights' battle had spread to other railroads. On March 1, the railroads began efforts to run the blockades. Alvarado, Palestine and Denison were the scenes of clashes between strikers and railroad officials attempting to move trains.

In Fort Worth the Knights, in company with friends and workers of similar persuasion, halted all rail traffic. Railroad ties were stacked on the rails to keep trains in the yards. A Missouri Pacific train taking the state adjutant general and other officials to the disturbance at Alvarado was stopped at the depot. More than two thousand residents gathered in the yards. Several arrests were made, but the train was held through the next day.

The Austin Statesman reported:

> Fort Worth is in the hands of the mob. The citizens' posse, summoned by the sheriff to assemble this morning at the Missouri Pacific Yards, met some 300 strong, according to orders. Most of the citizens were unarmed. About 400 strikers, armed, desperate, and ready for bloodshed, were on the scene. Fifty well-armed officers were also on hand. A freight train was made up, and the Missouri Pacific engine came along to pull out the train. A grand rush was made by the strikers for the engine. Arms were presented on both sides. The engine was not molested, but all the cars were uncoupled, and even the nuts were taken out of the draw heads. Some of the Knights were arrested, and the engine was sent back to the house, and all attempts to move trains abandoned.

Three days later, an effort was made to move a freight train to Alvarado. The ranks of law officers were increased to help control the situation. Courtright was named acting U.S. deputy marshal; he also was appointed deputy sheriff of Johnson County in case trouble should occur there.

With the law officers aboard, the engine was backed through the Fort Worth yards to pick up some coal cars at Hodge.[27] The switch yards were jammed with strikers, officers, and spectators; no effort was made to stop the train. Switches were spiked to prevent their being thrown. The train came back through the yards with only a minor incident; a woman waving a red flag stepped onto the tracks. The train did not reduce speed. She was pulled clear at the last moment by a companion. The train traveled on southward.

Apparently no serious trouble was expected outside the yards. There was not a single rifle aboard the train. All five officers, including Courtright, were armed only with pistols.

As the train approached Buttermilk Junction,[28] the engineer noticed that a switch had been thrown. Four men were seen walking away from the tracks. The train was brought to a stop. Courtright swung down from the cab and ordered the four men to halt. The officers left the train, searched the men, and found them unarmed. They were escorting them back to the train when five more men were sighted in the high grass along the edge of a gully a hundred yards away. Well beyond effective pistol range, they were armed with Winchesters. They obviously were preparing to use them.

Courtright called out to them: "For God's sake, don't shoot!"

The answer was a volley from the rifles. Tarrant County Deputy Sheriff Dick Townsend fell fatally wounded. Not only were the officers outgunned, but they also were caught in a crossfire. Another batch of riflemen—none of the officers could tell how many—opened fire from behind a pile of lumber near the tracks in front of the train. During the next 15 minutes, an estimated 100 rounds were fired. Officer Charlie Sneed was shot through the face. Another officer received a minor wound. Two bullets passed through Courtright's hat.

The train was backed into Union Station. News of the gunfight at Buttermilk Junction spread rapidly.

The *Fort Worth Gazette* reported the following day:

> Rumors of the most sensational character were rife in early portions of last night. Nearly every male citizen of the town was armed and prepared for trouble. It was reported that the strikers intended to raid the gun stores and burn the Union depot. It is also said that they threatened to clear the city of "scabs" within three days. Sheriff Maddox has arranged to give three taps continuously of the fire bell as a danger signal. The strikers, it is understood, use the Santa Fe switch engine for the same purpose. It is safe to say that two thousand citizens are now bearing arms, and if another collision occurs it will, in all probability, result in a more serious loss of life than that of yesterday.

Mayor John Peter Smith sent a wire to Governor John Ireland: "We are threatened with serious trouble here. The presence of one or two companies of Rangers or state militia would prevent a riot. Can you furnish the troops? Answer."

The governor replied that two companies of Rangers were on the way from Austin under command of the adjutant general; another company was dispatched from Harrold on a special train. Two companies—more than 70 officers—were ordered to Fort Worth from Dallas.

That evening the *Fort Worth Gazette* reported:

> The city is very quiet at this midnight hour. About the Union depot squads of citizens armed with repeating rifles and shotguns, patrol the platform. There is no loud talk or bluster. No strikers are to be seen. The Knights of Labor were in council, but what they did is unknown outside the order . . . Some predict further trouble today, while others are inclined to the opinion that the worst has already happened, and that no further bloodshed will ensue.

Few of the strikers who took part in the gunfight at Buttermilk Junction were identified. Thomas Nace, a young railroad man, later was treated by a doctor for a gunshot wound; he admitted that he had received it in the battle. He was lodged in the county jail. Frank Pierce, who operated a downtown peanut stand, was seen wielding a rifle among the strikers during the battle. His body was found the next day on the prairie at the edge of town. His death remained a mystery.

Much of the resentment against the railroad in the affair was focused on Courtright. The *San Antonio Light* commented in an editorial: "Jim Courtright is largely responsible for the Fort Worth massacre; but who is responsible for Jim Courtright?"

His appointment as a law officer was widely questioned. Mayor John Peter Smith replied to critics with the observation that those who violated the law had no right to choose who should arrest them.

Most of Fort Worth's animosity toward Courtright stemmed not from the fact that he was well-deputized, but that he was admittedly in the pay of, and acting on orders from the railroad.

Governor Ireland arrived in Fort Worth and conferred with city officials. State troops were used to help move trains. Apparently they also were ordered to assist in protecting Courtright from angry Fort Worth residents. The *Fort Worth Gazette* reported:

> Governor Ireland . . . declared that he had never ordered out the militia except in cases of extreme necessity, and in referring to the criticism aroused by his ordering the Rangers here to guard Courtright (whose life had been threatened by the mob), gave an explanation of that circumstance. He said the attorney general, who was a passenger on the train, saw the mob congregating around the depot, and arriving at Austin, reported the condition of affairs to him officially. On the basis of this he ordered the Rangers here to report for duty to the sheriff.

Courtright continued to operate his detective agency in Fort Worth until gambler Luke Short put an end to his colorful career on February 8, 1887.

Short, who owned the gambling concession at the White Elephant Saloon, 308-310 Main Street, and Courtright had been acquaintances for many years. Short's reputation as a gunfighter was on a par with that of Courtright. But there were mysterious aspects in his erratic career.

Short's family came to Texas during the Civil War. The general impression was that they were from Arkansas. Short went up the trail to Kansas several times during his youth, working for various traildrivers. In Kansas, he discovered that the life of a gambler could be much easier than that of a cowboy. He practiced his trade in cattle towns and mining camps throughout the West during the next few years. In Leadville, Colorado, he killed a local badman in a celebrated gunfight. In Tombstone, Arizona, he faced and killed a well known gunman, Charley Storms. He returned to Dodge City, Kansas, where he was connected with the gambling ring concession protected by Bat Masterson, Wyatt Earp, et al. . . . A vigilante committee broke up the clique, and Short drifted on to Fort Worth.

No disagreement was known to exist between Short and Courtright. The gunfight flared with a suddenness that stunned Fort Worth.

Short's partner, Jake Johnson, was the only close witness to the battle. His account and that of Short jibed in essential details.

Johnson said that he was talking with Courtright on the sidewalk in front of the White Elephant when a subject arose that led him to summon Luke Short, who was in the saloon having his shoes blackened. The three strolled about a half a block from the saloon, and stood talking in front of Ella Blackwell's shooting gallery.

As the three men talked, Short's thumbs were hooked in the armholes of his vest. He lowered his hands suddenly, and Courtright said, "Don't pull any gun on me."

"I have no gun there," Short said, making a movement as if to pull up his vest. At the gesture, Courtright went for his gun. Short drew a .45 Colt's revolver from his hip and fired. His first bullet shattered Courtright's "hammer thumb" as Courtright's pistol cleared the holster. Before Courtright could toss the pistol to his other hand, Short fired three more times. Each bullet took effect. Courtright died a few minutes later.

The exact relationship of Courtright and Short was a matter of much speculation. Although Short said in his testimony that "there is no reason to refrain from telling how it happened," his account of the crucial conversation is a study in vagueness:

> Early in the evening I was getting my shoes blackened at the White Elephant, when a friend of mine asked me if there was any trouble between Courtright and myself, and I told him there was nothing. A few minutes later I was at the bar with a couple of friends when someone called me. I went out into the vestibule and saw Jim Courtright and Jake Johnson. Jake and I had talked for a while that evening on a subject in which Jim's name was mentioned, but no idea of a difficulty was entertained. I walked out with them upon the sidewalk, and we had some quiet talk on private affairs. I reminded him of some past transactions, not in an abusive or reproachful manner, to which he assented, but not in a very cordial way.

It was at this point, Short said, that he made the gesture which Courtright apparently misinterpreted.

Johnson's testimony was no more revealing on the subject of the conversation.

There were reports that Courtright was "shaking down" Short for protection. The *Dallas Morning News* subscribed to this theory:

> While Courtright was a refugee from New Mexican justice, certain parties [in Fort Worth] interested themselves to have Courtright return for the alleged purpose of putting Luke Short out of the way. Courtright came back, but the scheme miscarried, and was dropped, but Courtright still remembered what he was brought back for. After gambling was opened up in Fort Worth, Courtright, so it is said, exacted a certain sum each month as an inducement for him and his detective aid [sic] to keep their mouths shut. This was paid regularly according to all accounts. Recently keno had been running, Short being the head of it, and Courtright wanted a certain sum from that game. Short refused to put up, and it is claimed that Courtright made threats to make Short bite the dust.

Others said that Short had been fleecing too many of Fort Worth's young men at the keno tables, and that a group of wealthy merchants had hired Courtright to curb Short's operations. Some said that Short was interested in Betty Courtright; one who said so was Betty Courtright. She later told her family that immediately after the shooting Short came to her, expressed his regrets, and said he would like to atone for the killing by marrying her and taking care of her children. She said she told him that his condolences could best be expressed in some other manner, and ran him off with a shotgun.

Courtright's funeral was the largest Fort Worth had ever seen; the procession of carriages to the graveyard was six blocks in length.

The slaying of Courtright, and the attendant nationwide publicity, again focused Fort Worth's concern on Hell's Half Acre. Newspapers long had published accounts of the Acre's murders and robberies, along with heart-rending stories of suicides among the Acre's "fallen angels." Courtright's death came in the midst of a new wave of robberies and shootings. Amid the violence was a case that came to be known as the Crucifixion of Sally. A prostitute known only as Sally was found dead one morning, nailed to the wall of an outhouse. The crime was never solved, and it left a good portion of the town horrified.

Mayor H. S. Broiles and County Attorney R. L. Carlock led a new campaign to clean up Hell's Half Acre.

Broiles and the City Council began by creating a permanent police force in 1887. Fees of office were abolished in favor of set salaries for city officials, removing some of the temptation for bribery. Strict regulations were enacted for the police department; most significantly, policemen were forbidden to leave their beats to enter houses of prostitution, variety theaters, or saloons except in the line of duty. By 1889, Hell's Half Acre was virtually closed. For more than a decade, Fort Worth was relatively quiet.

Then, just before the turn of the century, Hell's Half Acre emerged in a new area—from Thirteenth to Seventeenth Street, and from Main to Jones. Again, most of the activity was centered along Rusk Street.

Along about 1898, a handsome, well-dressed young man began spending considerable time in Hell's Half Acre. He was known as "Jim Lowe." He seemed to have plenty of money. He also had many friends who drifted through town to visit him. They partied a lot.

Only a few residents of Hell's Half Acre knew that "Jim Lowe" was not his real name. Even fewer knew that the name under his pictures on the "wanted" posters, "Butch Cassidy," was not the right one, either.

He was born George Leroy Parker in Circle Valley, Utah, in 1866. As a teenager, he came under the influence of an outlaw, Mike Cassidy, who worked for a while on the Parker ranch. Cassidy taught young George to handle a gun, and took him along on some horse-stealing expeditions. Cassidy later went to Mexico and was killed in a gunfight. George Parker had a "falling out" with his father. When he left the ranch, he disowned his father's name and called himself George Cassidy. Later, he worked for a while in a butcher shop and acquired the nickname "Butch."

He worked as a mule skinner in the boom town of Telluride, Colorado. In 1886, he became a member of the McCarty gang—a family group following in the footsteps of the James and Younger Brothers. Cassidy learned the art of robbing trains and banks. In 1890, Tom McCarty announced that the gang was moving into Oregon. Cassidy elected to stay behind. He worked for various ranches, mixing the life of a cowboy with occasional horse stealing forays. In 1894, a missing herd of 30 horses was traced to Cassidy through letters he had written to his girl. At the trial, Cassidy's lawyer produced a bill of sale for the horses. Unfortunately, the man whose name was forged on the document happened to be in town. Cassidy was sentenced to five years in the Wyoming State Penitentiary.

In 1895, Cassidy was paroled by Governor William A. Richards on the promise that Cassidy would never again molest the state of Wyoming. Cassidy kept his word. The governor of Utah reportedly later told Richards, "I sure wish you had included Utah."

During the next few years, Cassidy assembled the largest gang of outlaws ever to work in the West. Although they became known as the "Hole in the Wall Gang," Cassidy and his followers used many hideouts—Powder Springs,

Hole in the Wall, Robber's Roost, and Brown's Hole, among others. Eventually, they came to be known as the "Wild Bunch." In operation, the Wild Bunch was a loose confederation of several gangs; a bandit who took part in one robbery might choose to skip the next. After each "raise," the bandits scattered like quail, leaving the scene by different routes to reassemble later.

In 1898, their headquarters in effect was moved to Fannie Porter's house in Hell's Half Acre, Fort Worth.[29]

While posses combed their area of operations in the Northern Plains states, the outlaws met at Fannie Porter's, partied, and planned their next "raise." The friends who came to see "Jim Lowe" in Fort Worth were Harry Longbaugh, better known as "The Sundance Kid"; Harry Tracy, Harvey Logan, better known as "Kid Curry"; Sam and "Blackjack" (Tom) Ketchum, Elza Lay, Deaf Charley Hanks, Ben Kilpatrick, and Bill Carver.

Once, in a party mood, some of the Wild Bunch donned their best attire and posed for pictures in a Fort Worth photographer's studio.

Celebrating one successful "raise," Bill Carver and Kid Curry visited Fort Worth night spots with two of Fannie Porter's girls, Lillie Davis and Maud Walker. In a burst of enthusiasm, Bill Carver and Lillie Davis were married. The four partied at Maddox Flats, 1014½ Main Street, for five days. Then the newly married couple went to Houston on a wedding trip. When they returned, Fannie Porter gave the bridal party. During the revelry, Butch Cassidy rode a bicycle through the streets of Hell's Half Acre while his friends and their girls yelled encouragement.

After a trip to Colorado and Idaho, Carver sent Lillie home to Palestine, Texas, explaining only that he was "going up the road." That was the last Lillie saw of him. Carver was killed by Concho County Sheriff E. S. Briant in a gunfight on the streets of Sonora. Lillie Davis returned to work at Fannie Porter's place.

In the winter of 1900-1901, a new girl came to work at Fannie Porter's. She was known as Etta Place. Her background was a mystery.[30] The Sundance Kid fell in love with her. Apparently his affection was returned.

Butch Cassidy was growing increasingly concerned over the future of the Wild Bunch. The Union Pacific had hired the Pinkerton Detective Agency to put a stop to their train robberies. The Pinkerton Agency also had among its clients various bankers' associations. William Pinkerton made the capture of the Wild Bunch a personal project. He assembled his best agents from throughout the world. He added to his payroll some of the most famous law officers in the West. At the regional headquarters in Denver, Pinkerton operatives followed the feats of the Wild Bunch with red flags on a master map. They were beginning to fathom the Wild Bunch's methods. The ranks were growing thin. "Flat-Nosed George" Curry was cornered by a posse in Utah and lost a desperate fight for his life. Lonny Logan, the younger brother of Harvey Logan, was tracked down and killed by a Pinkerton-directed posse at his home in Missouri. Sam Ketchum was fatally wounded after a train robbery in New Mexico and died in prison. "Blackjack" (Tom) Ketchum attempted to rob a train in New Mexico alone, was riddled with buckshot, surrendered, and was hanged in Clayton. Elza Lay was captured in New Mexico and sentenced to life in prison.

In Fort Worth, Cassidy knew that his luck was running out. He long had thought of taking his talents to South America. But Kid Curry was trying to talk him into one more "raise." The Sundance Kid said he would not take part; he now had other interests. Kid Curry eventually convinced Cassidy, who figured he would need more money for his South America trip.

Cassidy, the Sundance Kid, and Etta Place left Fort Worth by train for New York. Cassidy planned to see them off for South America, then head west for his final robbery in the United States.

In New York they stayed in a fashionable rooming house, shopped at Tiffany's, dined in the best restaurants, and attended the outstanding shows in town, including one starring Lillian Russell. At De Young's, a photographic salon located in Matthew Brady's old studio, they had their pictures made.

Cassidy received a letter from Kid Curry, setting the time and place for the last robbery. Etta Place and Sundance left for South America. Cassidy traveled west for the big "raise;" it took place at Wagner, Montana, on July 3, 1901. The target was a Great Northern train carrying $40,000 in nonnegotiable currency, en route from the U.S. Treasury to two Helena banks. After the holdup, the Wild Bunch scattered and returned by various routes to Fort Worth.

Most of the money was in unsigned notes, lacking only the signatures of the presidents and cashiers of the banks to become legal tender. The more literate girls among those at Fannie Porter's place helped with the signatures. A few days later, a Dallas bank teller discovered one of the forged notes. He notified Pinkerton. But the net closed on Fort Worth too late. Cassidy had left for South America.

Cassidy, Longbaugh and Etta Place lived as respectable ranchers in Argentina for almost five years. But after a time, the Pinkerton operatives put the puzzle together. They talked with Fannie Porter, the clerk at Tiffany's, Mrs. Julia Thompson, who managed the New York boarding house, and various members of the gang who had wound up behind bars. Frank Dimaio, one of the best detectives in the Pinkerton organization, was dispatched to Argentina. He distributed "wanted" posters throughout South America. The posters utilized the photographs made in Fort Worth and New York.

Word of the posters reached the fugitives ahead of Dimaio. Leaving the ranch, Cassidy, Longbaugh and Etta Place moved into the interior and began robbing village banks. Etta Place held the horses.

In 1906, Etta Place became ill with recurring attacks of appendicitis. She feared the probability of surgery under the region's primitive conditions. The Sundance Kid brought her back to the United States. They sailed from Buenos Aires to London, and then to New York. The operation was performed in Denver. While Etta Place was in the hospital, the Sundance Kid went on a marathon drunk. At one point, he shot a policeman in the leg. On sobering, he sent Etta Place some money, and fled back to South America.

Cassidy and Longbaugh continued the robberies in the back country. In 1911, they robbed the mule train of the Alpoca Silver Mine and escaped with the payroll. They made the mistake of also taking the mule carrying the payroll—a huge, well branded animal that belonged to the mine superintendent. It was well known throughout the area. In the small *barrio* of San Vicente, Bolivia, a peace officer recognized the mule. He notified a detachment of the Bolivian cavalry, camped less than a mile away.

In the first exchange of gunfire, two troopers were killed. Longbaugh was wounded. The two outlaws barricaded themselves in a small hut. The gunbattle lasted until darkness. Longbaugh bled to death during the night. Just before dawn, Cassidy killed himself with his last bullet.

Etta Place may or may not have returned to Fort Worth.[31] On her release from the hospital in Denver, she simply disappeared.

The activities of the Wild Bunch in Fort Worth were known outside Hell's Half Acre only to the Pinkerton agents and a few law officers, but there were other matters of public knowledge that again built pressure for reform.

The murder of County Attorney Jeff McLean concentrated considerable ire on the Acre. A leader in a crusade against open gambling, McLean was returning from a drive with his wife on March 21, 1907, when he saw Sheriff T. J. Wood and several deputies conducting a raid on William Tomlinson's gambling room near Sixth and Main. McLean parked his buggy and went in to assist the deputies, who were removing the confiscated gambling equipment. In returning to his buggy, McLean was stopped by Tomlinson, who whipped out a pistol and killed him with one shot. Many members of the Texas Legislature were in town for the Fat Stock Show. Shocked reactions to the slaying helped in the passage of a state law against gambling.

In 1909, an effort was made to confine Hell's Half Acre to a "reservation," bordered by Fourteenth and Eleventh, and Calhoun and Grove. A later effort to move the "reservation" to the Riverside area failed when that section was destroyed by fire.

Many factors combined in the last sustained effort to clean up Hell's Half Acre. Not the least of them was the attention devoted to the area by one of the most controversial men who ever lived in Fort Worth, the Reverend J. Frank Norris.

Reared in poverty in East Texas, Norris in his formative years had witnessed the tragic effect of liquor on his father, and the strength that his mother found in her religion. He also had known violence; at 15, he was shot by horse thieves. He was completely paralyzed for three years. At 18, after his recovery, he told his mother that he was convinced that "God has laid His hand on me to preach the Gospel." Through years of hard work, Norris managed to attend Baylor University. His energy and drive eventually were recognized. He rose to the pulpit of one of Dallas' largest churches. He then became editor of the *Baptist Standard,* a position that landed him in his first major controversy.

Norris used the *Standard* to crusade against racetrack gambling. Some church members felt that the campaign was the liveliest thing that had happened to the church in years. Others felt that the furor raised in the state's newspapers by the *Standard's* outspoken editorials was merely cheap publicity for the *Standard,* and that the issue should have been beneath the official notice of the church.

As was his habit, Norris put all his energies into the crusade. His health deteriorated. After the long, successful battle, he resigned as editor of the *Standard.*

Norris then received a call to the First Baptist Church in Fort Worth. He accepted. His ministry during the first two years was quiet. But Norris was spiritually discontent. He said of those years:

> I was the most knocked down, run over, chewed up, fired preacher in the world . . . . I was drawing a big salary, wearing tailor made suits, preaching in the midst of a city of over a hundred thousand people, none paying any attention to me . . . . I was not causing a riffle. My moisture was turned into the drought of summer, my soul was poured out like water. I was unfaithful to my Heavenly-committed trust . . . . Something had to happen . . . . Never in all my life did I go through such heart searching.

Norris reflected on his tenure as editor of the *Baptist Standard.* He decided that if sensationalism achieved results, then he would have sensationalism.

He placed display advertisements in the *Fort Worth Record* — the first paid church advertisements in the city's history. Each week, he announced a sermon topic designed to pack the church, such as: *Why Dallas Beat Fort Worth In Baseball*. (The answer, after dramatic buildup: "Dallas beat Fort Worth because Dallas was better prepared for the game. Boys, you had better get prepared for the game of life!").

Many church members preferred a quieter worship theme. Strong opposition developed against Norris' methods. Then, in 1911, a statewide prohibition effort was launched in a convention at Waco. Norris pledged the campaign his full support. Immediately afterward, the state retail liquor dealers called a meeting in Fort Worth's Northside Coliseum to plan an effective counter-campaign. Prominent among Fort Worth residents on promotion and entertainment committees for the dealers' convention were three deacons in Norris' congregation.

Norris had no room in his mind for compromise on the issue of liquor. He rallied support, and summoned his church board. He demanded that the three deacons resign publicly from the board. He warned that if they did not, he would request the church to expel them from membership during the next morning's worship. The three deacons and all of Norris' opponents walked out of the meeting in a body. They did not return to the church. Six hundred members left the congregation within the next few weeks, taking most of the church income with them.

Yet, Norris packed the church each Sunday; new crowds came to hear his colorful brand of evangelism.

"Something happened to the church besides the row," Norris said. "The Lord came around and paid us a visit. And folks came. And salvation came."

In search of more ammunition for his sermons, Norris found a theme close to home. Hell's Half Acre still remained one of the largest and most aggressive vice zones in the Southwest.

The Tarrant County General Pastors' Association earlier in 1911 had agreed to campaign for the closing of the zone. A committee of ten laymen and ten pastors was named to assemble information on the Acre. J. Frank Norris, at 35, was the youngest member of the committee.

The panel hired a private investigator, George Chapman, to gather evidence. He soon returned with the details behind the operation of 80 houses of prostitution. With growing concern, the church leaders learned that eight of the largest houses were owned by men prominent and influential in civic affairs and on boards of many of the congregations represented. After considerable discussion, the committee voted to prosecute the violators, but only after "each pastor had been given time to work out the situation in his own congregation."

Most members of the committee lost enthusiasm for the project. Norris did not.

"The arrangement was that each minister would get up the following Sunday night and read out publicly the names of the owners of those houses of ill repute," he said. "You understand this agreement was entered into before we found out who the men were. But I, being young and unsophisticated, thought the other brethren would carry out their part of the agreement. Therefore, I proceeded to read the names."

Norris' action ensured a full church for the next several Sundays. He utilized the opportunity by preparing some of the most sensational sermons he ever preached. He linked Fort Worth's shortcomings with the biblical themes of fallen daughters, prodigal sons, Sodom and Gomorrah and the Judgment Day. His topics no longer were mere gimmicks. Sermon titles such as *The Ten Biggest Devils in Town and Their Records Given* were supported by sensational material gleaned from Chapman's investigations.

His sermons split Fort Worth into two camps just as they had earlier divided his church. On one Saturday evening, two shots were fired through the window of Norris' study, narrowly missing the pastor as he sat at his desk preparing a sermon.

By the summer of 1911, his congregations were so large that he bought an old circus tent which had been used by Sarah Bernhardt on her national tours. It was erected between Throckmorton and Houston on Tenth Street, and Norris began a 90-day revival, with services each evening.

Six days before the July 20 balloting on the liquor question, city firemen chopped down Norris' tent, declaring it a safety hazard. The "drys" lost the election by 6,000 votes, but Norris won a new theme. Turning his attention to the sins he saw in the city's administration, he continued his revival in the open air.

New fuel unexpectedly was provided by State Comptroller W. P. Lane, who announced that $400,000 in tax revenue could not be accounted for by the Fort Worth city administration. Norris focused his sermons on the city officials and the missing funds.

Mayor W. D. Davis called a mass meeting to answer Norris' charges. He requested that every adult male in town attend, but "no boys under twenty-one and no women." The mayor spoke for two hours, reportedly concluding with the observation that "if there are fifty red-blooded men in this town, a preacher will be hanging from the lamp post before daylight."

Norris sent a male stenographer to the meeting. The full minutes of what occurred were printed in a small newspaper, *Xray,* under a simple heading: "LIARS".

On January 11, 1912, Norris' church was damaged by fire. Norris did not slacken his campaign. On February 4, the church was destroyed in a night-time blaze. On the same evening, a burning bundle of oiled rags was tossed onto the porch of Norris' home at 810 West Fifth Street. That fire was extinguished without damage.

After an investigation, Norris was charged with burning the church. The month-long trial was almost as emotional and sensational as Norris' own sermons. He was acquitted. After the verdict was returned, his supporters sang hymns in the courtroom.

Norris' campaign against Hell's Half Acre was not entirely successful. References to the section acknowledged its existence as late as March of 1917. Statistics showed that 60 per cent of the arrests for such crimes as robbery, fighting, assault, and murder occurred there. But efforts were continued by the city's successive administrations, the growing prohibition forces, religious organizations, and women's clubs. Various vice-oriented establishments persisted, but Hell's Half Acre eventually ceased to exist as an entity, and faded into Fort Worth's history.

NOTES, A BUNCH OF WILDNESS

23. Rusk Street, named for General Thomas Jefferson Rusk, developed such a bad reputation that Fort Worth residents eventually felt that it conveyed little honor to the hero of San Jacinto. The name of the street was changed in 1917 to a more appropriate appellation, "Commerce."

24. The site of Courtright's farm has been located as near present-day Oakwood Cemetery.

25. During the Red Light's existence, one third of all arrests for major crimes took place within its walls.

26. The estimate of the number of guns drawn was made by Dallas and Fort Worth newspapers. All printed details of the affair.

27. Located in the southeast portion of Fort Worth, the hamlet of Hodge — and the name — has passed from existence.

28. Buttermilk Junction, then well out in the country, was near the 2200 block of South Main Street.

29. Fannie Porter and a number of her girls later gave signed statements to William Pinkerton, who had pursued the Wild Bunch all over the West. The statements reposed in the files of the Pinkerton Detective Agency until the early 1950s, when the material was made available to writer James D. Horan. The material in Horan's subsequent book, "The Wild Bunch," revealed to the public for the first time that Hell's Half Acre in Fort Worth had been the gang's primary hideout.

30. Frank Dimaio, who pursued Cassidy, Longbaugh and Etta Place to the end, once said he had evidence to believe that she had been a school teacher in Denver.

31. After a column by the author appeared in the *Fort Worth Star-Telegram,* pointing out the parallels between fact and the movie, *Butch Cassidy and the Sundance Kid,* the author was visited by a Pinkerton detective to ascertain the source of some of the information. The detective explained: "The file has never been closed on Etta Place." If alive, she now would be in the neighborhood of 90. On October 25, 1970, the *Fort Worth Press* published a story by Delbert Willis speculating as to whether Etta Place became Eunice Gray, who operated the well-known Waco Hotel, 110½ E. 15th, for more than 40 years. The story observed parallels in ages, and the fact that Eunice Gray mentioned spending time in South America. Eunice Gray was burned to death in a fire at the hotel on January 26, 1962. She was 77. Her estate was valued at $90,000.

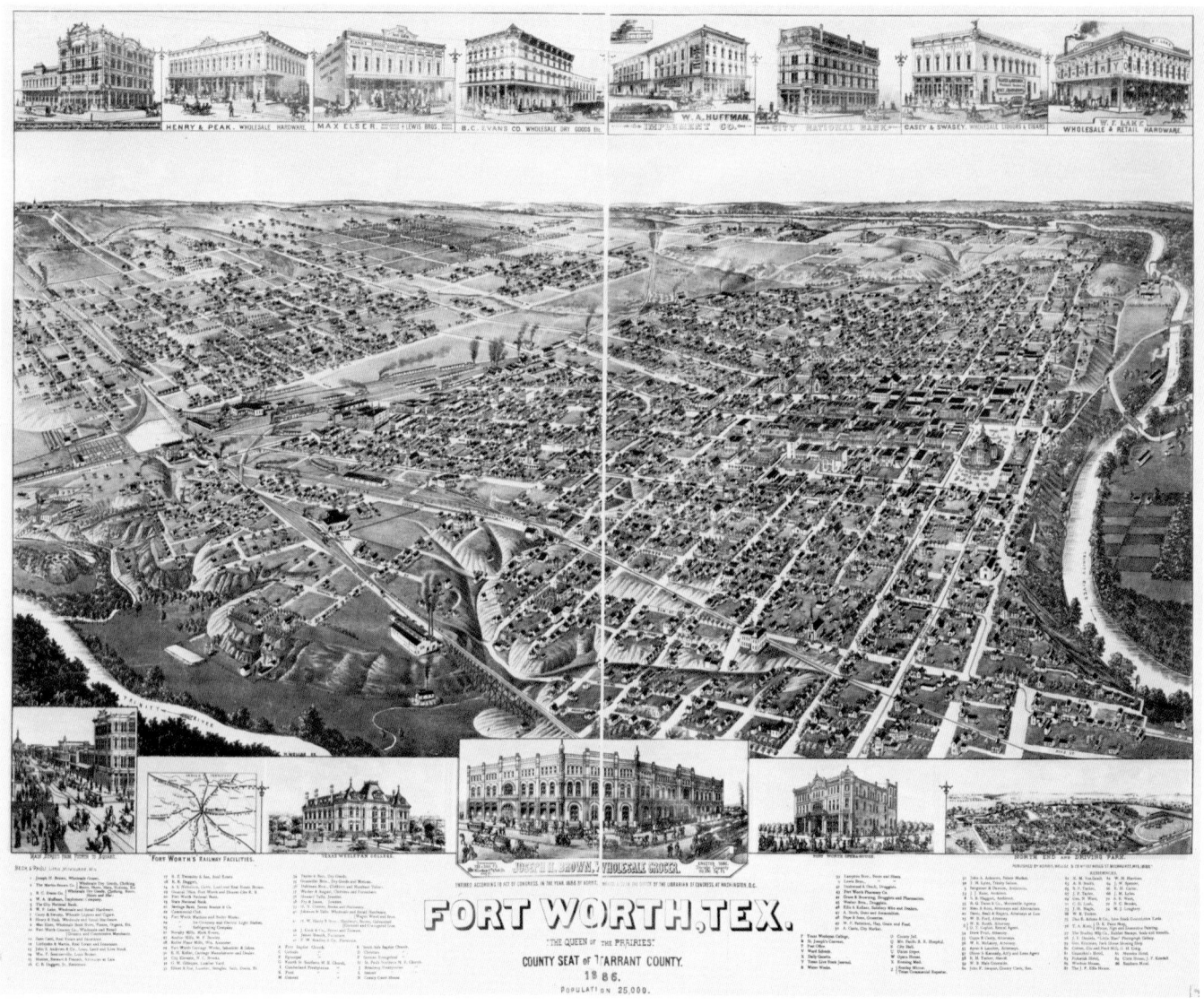

33. This 1886 city view of Fort Worth shows the considerable amount of progress made in the decade after the first lithographic city view of Fort Worth was made. (See frontispiece.) Because of the detailed identifications at the bottom of the print it is a good key to the "Queen of the Prairies." Courtesy Library of Congress, Washington, D.C.

34. An unknown photographer captured this Houston Street scene in 1876. Some of the buildings were beginning to show signs of wear even by this early date. Next door to Tivoli Hall is A. J. Anderson's Gun Store, and further down the block is Fakes & Company, a furniture store. Courtesy *Fort Worth Star-Telegram*.

35. This early view of Fort Worth from the courthouse square shows Rusk Street in the foreground, Belknap Street on the left, and Weatherford Street on the right. Rusk Street was changed to Commerce Street when the street acquired such a reputation that the city fathers felt it dishonored General Thomas J. Rusk, hero of the Texas Revolution, to have the street named for him.   Courtesy W. D. Smith, Fort Worth.

36. Land agency building, located on the corner of Lancaster and Main. As Fort Worth grew, land speculators bought up the surrounding prairies. Courtesy Fort Worth Public Library.

37. Pat Morrison, Deputy Sheriff of Tarrant County. Courtesy Mrs. Joseph J. Minton, Fort Worth.

38. The famous "Hole in the Wall" gang often used Fort Worth as their "hideout" between jobs. On one occasion in December, 1900, they had their picture made by a Fort Worth photographer named Schwartz. The film, *Butch Cassidy and the Sundance Kid*, contained a scene in which the gang posed for their picture. That scene was based on this authentic photograph. Standing, left to right, are Bill Carver and Harvey Logan. Seated, left to right, are Harry Longbaugh ("The Sundance Kid"), Ben Kilpatrick, and George Parker ("Butch" Cassidy). Courtesy Western History Collections, University of Oklahoma Library, Norman.

39. The railroad strike of 1886 was perhaps the bitterest labor dispute Fort Worth has known. Begun by the Knights of Labor in an effort to break Jay Gould's stranglehold on the country's railroads, the strike spread to Fort Worth on March 1. The nationwide strike ended a month later. From left to right: Will Owens, Henry Putts, J. C. Barringer, Sam Pickett, Charles Kuhley, G. H. Clark, J. R. Robinson, Corp. J. W. Durbin, Lt. A. C. Grimes, Capt. G. H. Schmitt of the Texas Rangers. Courtesy Western History Collections, University of Oklahoma Library, Norman.

40. Texas & Pacific hired armed guards to protect valuable shipments from train robbers such as the Wild Bunch. Courtesy Mrs. A. G. McDaniel, Fort Worth.

41. Anheuser-Busch Brewing Association, 1111 Lamar Street, Fort Worth. About 1905.
Courtesy Fort Worth Public Library.

42. David Boaz built the first two-story home in Fort Worth at 611 East Bluff Street in 1872. Courtesy Fort Worth Public Library.

43. The man who received much of the credit for cleaning up Hell's Half Acre was the Rev. J. Frank Norris, pastor of Fort Worth's First Baptist Church. Courtesy *Fort Worth Star-Telegram*.

IV. THE GOOD YEARS

44. Capt. Buckley B. Paddock. Courtesy Mrs. C. W. Hutchison, Fort Worth.

In the spring of 1884 Captain B. B. Paddock retired from active newspaper work. However, he retained a financial interest in publishing and in time became a historian and a commentator on his favorite subject, Fort Worth.

From his long observation of the development of the town, Paddock evolved an oft-stated theory which he perhaps best expressed in 1887:

> Refinement follows wealth according to the law of cause and effect, and social pleasures increase and multiply as refinement ploughs its way into rugged western life. This has been noticeable in the social status of Fort Worth during the last three years. At the beginning of that period, but little attention had been paid to the development or cultivation of social relations among the people.
>
> The previous seven years in the history of the city had been spent with everybody in pursuit of money. Many had scarcely expected to make Fort Worth a permanent home, and their minds occasionally went back to scenes of other days in other states. The border roughness was exhilarating in a business view but depressing in its social aspects.
>
> But the year 1883, with its era of public improvement, caused a revolution in social affairs. Homes were improved. The city began to have a finished appearance. Shrubbery and shade trees were cultivated. Men of wealth built costly residences. Sidewalks sprang into existence in all parts of the city which then was growing very rapidly.
>
> The churches increased in numbers. Their congregations swelled and the social garden budded and blossomed in proportion to the development of business enterprises. The roughness of frontier life was passing away. The city prospered. Everybody prospered, and life in Fort Worth commenced to adorn itself with comforts and delicacies.

Paddock's observations were proved astute. These changes he recorded in 1887 continued to gather momentum through the 1890s. Economic gains from long years of hard work were assimilated, and Fort Worth arrived at a quieter, more serene way of life. In education, public facilities, cultural pursuits and personal comforts, Fort Worth made great strides in less than two decades.

Yet, Paddock may have been modest on Fort Worth's earliest efforts toward refinement.

The first opera house, Evans Hall, was opened to the public shortly after the coming of the railroad in 1876. For the most part, it presented traveling shows and revues. But grand opera arrived two years later with the Adah Richmond English Opera Troupe, consisting of forty singers, an orchestra and chorus. The company presented *Les Cloches de Cornerville* for its first night performance and *La Perichole* on the second night. Although these were the first professional opera productions ever staged in Fort Worth, the town may not have been as backward, musically, as some assumed. When the Tagliapietra Grand Italian Opera Company faced bad weather and a small house in Fort Worth two years later, the planned production of *La Favorita* was replaced at the last moment with the shorter *Martha,* with parts omitted. The Fort Worth audience recognized the insult to its intelligence. The *Fort Worth Democrat* warned, "Companies who do not intend to do their best are advised to stay away from Fort Worth."

In August of 1882, a long, complicated battle with opponents was ended and a property tax of half of one per cent was voted to support free public schools. Vacant houses and churches were used while permanent school buildings were under construction. In February of 1883, twenty-one teachers began classes for an average attendance of 800 students. In the fall of that year 1,200 students met for classes in eight new buildings. Seven more teachers were added to the school system, providing twenty-four for white students and four for black.

Also in 1883, Fort Worth completed its first water system. An outbreak of typhoid fever in 1881 had prompted the appointment of Dr. H. W. Moore as the city's first health officer. In the summer of 1882, an epidemic of smallpox swept through town. A pest house was erected three miles south of the city. Dr. Moore's first concern in halting the epidemic was the city's water supply, which came chiefly from cisterns and wells polluted by the run-off from outhouses and stables. A pump station was erected near the Courthouse; it lifted 4,000,000 gallons of untreated water a day from the Trinity into six miles of pipe. Four years later, ninety wells were drilled to supplement the supply.

Weatherford, Houston and Main Streets were macadamized in 1882, as were stretches of other downtown streets. The first sewer system was begun in the same year. By 1886, the city directory boasted, "Fort Worth is the only completely sewered city among her many sister cities of the state, having upwards of twenty miles of piping laid."

The first central fire station, on Main Steet between Eleventh and Twelfth, was opened in 1883. A 3,000-pound bell was placed in the fire station tower.[32] The office of fire chief became a paid position. Eleven alarm boxes were installed downtown at a cost of $2,450, providing the first electric fire-alarm system in the state.

The first full-time district court for Tarrant County was created in 1884. In that year, home delivery of mail began and a new county jail was built north of the Courthouse at a cost of $60,000.

The 1880s brought an end to the era of the trail drives. More than 150,000 cattle passed through Fort Worth in 1880. In the following year, the total was considerably less. By the end of the 1884 season, the Chisholm Trail was virtually closed; settlement had moved the open range needed for trail herds too far west. Many ranchers were beginning to breed cattle that carried more beef, but they were not as well structured for walking as the Longhorns. However, these shorthorn cattle needed less space to swing their horns; a greater number could be crowded into a railroad car.

Ranchers were turning to rail shipment. As Fort Worth lost the trail driving business, its position as a railroad center retained the close association with the cattle industry.

Fort Worth became the headquarters of West Texas cattlemen. Early in the 1880s the *Fort Worth Democrat* was selected to publish the *Live Stock Journal* for the Cattle Raisers Association of Northwest Texas, recording the names, marks, brands and location of members. Copies were distributed widely to assist in locating stolen cattle and strays. The association hired brand inspectors in 1883 and its influence grew. When the organization was expanded to become the Cattle Raisers Association of Texas a decade later, Fort Worth was selected as the headquarters. Many successful ranchers built homes in Fort Worth.

Plains Indians who led raids into North Texas as late as the 1860s came to Fort Worth by rail in the 1880s to negotiate grazing leases on tribal lands to the north of Red River. For two of these Indians, Paddock's "refinements" proved to be more dangerous than the war trail.

Comanche Chief Quanah Parker[33] and his uncle, Yellow Bear, arrived in Fort Worth on Saturday, December 19,.1885, to discuss overdue rent from leased reservation land with Captain J. Lee Hall, agent for the Kiowas, Comanches and Wichitas. They registered at The Pickwick, the most modern hotel the town offered. Yellow Bear retired early in the evening, and Quanah spent some time with George W. Briggs, the foreman of the Waggoner ranch.

Quanah returned to the room two hours later and went to bed.

In turning off the gaslight, he apparently did not close the valve completely. Fumes awakened him. Not realizing the gas was dangerous, he pulled the bedcover over his head and fell asleep. He awoke sick some time later, and aroused Yellow Bear. Both lost consciousness. Their plight was not discovered until almost 13 hours later. Yellow Bear was dead. Quanah had fallen near a window, and was gasping for breath.

A special delegation from Fort Worth went with Quanah and the body of Yellow Bear to Harrold, where they were met by Yellow Bear's relatives. The delegation wanted to be sure the Comanches understood the death was by accident. Quanah also was worried. He feared he would be blamed. He took with him a copy of the statement from the coroner's jury inquest, bearing an impressive seal. The chief also retained a lawyer to take depositions.

Electric lights replaced those gas jets a short time later. The first electric service franchise was issued by the city in 1885. Competition was keen.

Electric street lights and electric streetcars—replacing the "mule cars"—brought the most striking change to the appearance of the city. To some extent, the streetcar removed the horse and buggy from the streets.

In 1887, a syndicate bought eighty acres on the South Side from H. S. Leach. The price was $80,000. Leach had bought the land in 1870 for three dollars per acre. Known as the Fairmount Addition, the area was subdivided into graded lots and graveled streets. A streetcar line was formed by the syndicate to serve the section; power was supplied by an electric plant on the T&P Reservation.

The electric streetcar line, which began operation in 1889, was believed to be the first in Texas, and the second in the United States. Service was offered to nearly all sections of the South Side, populated or not. Companies later were formed for lines to other parts of the city. The cars often traversed open country. Drivers said that at night on some lonely stretches they heard the howling of wolves.

Streetcar riding became the thing to do. After making a young lady's acquaintance, a hopeful swain might suggest as a first date that he escort her on a streetcar ride on a Sunday afternoon. One Fort Worth resident, Albert S. Leach, said, "Many times I have seen ladies with evening gowns and gentlemen with tops and tails on the streetcar going to or coming from

Greenwall's Opera House when some of the stars of the Gay Nineties were here, or maybe a dance at the old Worth Hotel, which was quite a gathering place for both cattlemen and society."

Editor Paddock was instrumental in an effort to bring Fort Worth's affluence to national—and international—attention. Toronto, Canada, and St. Paul, Minnesota, were sponsoring "Ice Palaces" for amusement and exhibition purposes. Sioux City, Iowa, offered a "Corn Palace." The idea grew in Fort Worth that the town might provide what Paddock termed "an exhibition of the products of the field, forest, orchard and garden." This exhibition would be staged in the spring, the season "when there were no other places of entertainment and amusement anywhere in the country." Editor Paddock was named president of a company to raise an initial capital of $50,000, and Fort Worth's Spring Palace was born.

Paddock did not dally with words in describing the Spring Palace. He wrote, "It was easily the most beautiful structure ever erected on earth."

Many agreed. The fairy-castle exhibition hall on the Texas & Pacific Reservation was called "the pride and glory of Texas." The $100,000 building was constructed in the shape of a Saint Andrew's cross, with a massive dome 150 feet in diameter, surpassed in size only by the nation's Capitol. The building's fixtures were even more striking, and usually drew the most praise. Every inch of the 225-by-375-foot structure, with the exception of the floors, was blanketed with products of Texas artfully arranged to depict typical state scenes. Fort Worth women spent many long hours in decorating the interior with wheat, corn stalks, cactus, rye, moss, Johnson grass, cotton—every product imaginable. Shelled corn and oats covered the roofs of the 12 Moorish-styled towers. Strings of popcorn and peas curtained the windows.

No expense was spared in making Fort Worth's Spring Palace known throughout the nation. Special trains came from as far away as Boston and Chicago.

The Palace was opened May 10, 1889, with impressive ceremonies. The governor of Nebraska made the opening address and the Elgin Watch Factory Band of Elgin, Illinois, provided the music.

Fort Worth's expressed pride and affection for the Spring Palace reveals that it represented more than an exhibition hall. The Palace was a symbol of arrival after long years of hard work and constant growth.

This intrinsic aspect of the Palace made its loss an even greater tragedy.

Despite a large attendance, the first season of the Palace was not a financial success. A deficit of $23,000 was recorded that year. The directors easily raised the sum and made even more elaborate plans for the second season. The building was expanded by one hundred feet on each wing. Cities and counties from all over the state were assigned space and prizes were offered for the most attractive decorations. Paddock observed that the results were "very gratifying."

Fort Worth women were organized into ten groups, and each group worked eight and ten hours a day for more than one hundred days in decorating the building. Paddock wrote, "Such another example of patriotic purpose was never before seen in any community."

During the second season the Palace moved into the black financially. Paddock termed the year "profitable and successful from every standpoint."

The tragedy occurred on May 30, 1890. A dress ball was the scheduled attraction for the evening. It was next to the final night of the season. Special trains came from nearby cities and towns. More than 1,000 people came from Dallas. An estimated 7,000 people were in the building. Most were in the ballroom, where 16,000 square feet of space were devoted to dancing. The Elgin Watch Factory Band was again playing.

The structure suddenly was swept by fire. The origin was never ascertained. There were reports that a boy, "jigging for coins," stepped on a match. Flames shot up the dry moss, grass and straw decorations.

Paddock described the scene:

> In four minutes the building was a mass of flame, inside and out, and in eleven minutes the building fell to the ground. So rapid was the spread of the fire that the firemen, who were stationed in different parts of the building with their hoses connected to the fire hydrants, did not have time to turn on the water.
>
> Why hundreds did not perish is a mystery. The officials of the company, who were present, directed the visitors to the various exits, of which there were sixteen, and no Sunday school in the country was ever dismissed with more decorum and good order.
>
> That the loss of life was not appalling is one of the wonders of the occasion. About 30 people were injured, more or less seriously, and many were burned. Low-necked and short-sleeved dresses of the ladies exposed them to the falling cinders and pieces of the decorations which were of the lightest and most inflammable character.

One life was lost. Al Hayne, a native of England and a civil engineer, made repeated trips into the burning building. *Frank Leslie's Illustrated Newspaper* printed an account of his heroism for its nationwide audience. Frank Leslie's private railroad car was parked on a nearby railroad siding. The newspaper's quick-sketch artist recorded the scene, and a writer offered an eyewitness description:

> As the panic . . . increased, and it seemed probable that many would be burned to death, Mr. Hayne gave himself to the work of rescue. He picked up fainting women and terrified children, and dropped them out of the second story windows into willing arms waiting to receive them below. After all had left the building but Mr. Hayne and one woman, who had fainted, the flames enveloped the entire building. The fainting woman was several feet away from the window and her dress was already ablaze. The hero did not hesitate a moment, but ran to her, picked her up and, without a thought of self, leaped from the window with his senseless burden in his arms. His clothing was ablaze, and in the fall he broke several bones. He died three hours later, but his name will long be cherished as that of one who gave his life for others.[34]

> At the time of the fire Frank Leslie's special car, the Mayflower, was standing on the track directly opposite the Exposition grounds, and Mr. George E. Burr, the chief of the artist department of the Texas expedition of Leslie's, roused from his slumber by the cries of fire, hastily made, from the car platform, a sketch of the magnificent spectacle afforded by the burning buildings . . . The Mayflower was soon enveloped in smoke and cinders, and had not the wind been favorable the car would have been destroyed, or badly damaged.

Editorials and messages from throughout the country attempted to console Fort Worth on its loss. One of the most fitting was printed in *Frank Leslie's Illustrated Newspaper:* "Fort Worth is one of the most enterprising cities in Texas, and it is safe to say that even the destruction of its magnificent Spring Palace, which has attracted visitors from every section in the Union, will not dampen the ardor of its citizens nor lessen the magnificent prosperity which it rightfully enjoys."

The editorial was prophetic. Paddock's theory that "refinement follows wealth" prevailed. Fort Worth continued to assimilate the economic gains of the recent years. These efforts encompassed many facets.

Recreational facilities were expanded. Anticipating a boom in the wake of the Spring Palace, the H. B. Chamberlain Investment Company of Denver built Lake Como, southwest of the city, in 1889. A streetcar line was constructed through the desolate stretches to the lake pavilion. On the streetcar line, the company opened Arlington Inn, described in the 1893 *Baedeker's: A Handbook for Travellers* as "a winter-resort commanding a splendid view of the Trinity Valley." Rooms ranged from three to four dollars a night. The resort won a Baedeker asterisk of recommendation. Two serious setbacks drove the Denver firm into bankruptcy. The Arlington Inn was destroyed by fire in 1893, the same year that brought a financial panic.[35] Lake Como and the streetcar line were sold to other companies. Development of the region was delayed by several years, but the installations provided the basis for future growth.

In 1893 the Commissioners Court allocated $500,000 for a new courthouse to replace the structure erected after the fire in 1876. Work was completed in 1894. Voter concensus was that the new courthouse far exceeded anything Tarrant County would ever need. The commissioners were turned out of office in the next election for their extravagance.

Educational facilities were improved. Texas Wesleyan University had been founded in 1881; eight years later the name was changed to Fort Worth University. Within a decade, schools of law and medicine were added.[36] In 1910, Texas Christian University came "home" to Fort Worth. Two Disciples of Christ ministers, Addison and Randolph Clark, and their sister Ida had founded a one-room school in Fort Worth in 1869. Four years later, they moved the school to Thorp Spring in Hood County to get away from "the alluring vices of the city." Renamed Add-Ran College under church supervision, the school was moved to Waco in 1895. After a disastrous fire, Fort Worth brought the school "home" with the offer of a fifty-six-acre campus and $200,000 in cash. Southwestern Baptist Theological Seminary, founded in the Waco home of the Rev. B. H. Carroll, was moved to Fort Worth in 1910 after outgrowing its Waco facilities.

The Fort Worth Public Library Association was founded in April of 1892, and for six years the members worked to raise money for a good library. Twelve thousand dollars was all the group managed to collect. Mrs. D. B. Keeler set out to ask every man in town to donate the price of a good cigar. For good measure, she wrote to Andrew Carnegie, asking him to do the same. He responded with $50,000, and the library was built.

Merchandising assumed a more impressive tone. In 1882 a 24-year-old Tennessean, Jacob Washer, arrived and opened a store between Fourth and Fifth Streets on Houston. He soon teamed with Leopold August in partnership. Five years later August left to open his own store, A. and L. August Clothing Store. Nat Washer came to Fort Worth to join his brother in Washer Brothers. In 1889, William and George Monnig opened Monnig's between Twelfth and Thirteenth Streets. They lived on the second floor of the building during the first few years. W. C. Stripling, a young Bowie merchant, opened a branch store in Fort Worth in the early 1890s, using packing cases for counters. In 1904, H. C. Meacham opened a small drygoods store.

Hospital facilities were enlarged. St. Joseph's, opened in 1889, was supplemented by All Saints in 1895. City-County Hospital was established in 1907.

Fort Worth's first large hotel, the Worth, was built in 1894 at Seventh and Main.

Paddock's Tarantula Map became a complete reality, with railroad "legs" giving Fort Worth twelve trunk lines. The city's switchyards were handling 1,500,000 cars annually shortly after the turn of the century. Of the varied benefits from the railroads, perhaps the greatest was the packing plants.

Efforts were made as early as 1876 to pack meat in Fort Worth and to ship it by rail to Eastern markets. Facilities simply were not adequate for the meat to arrive in good condition. But by the late 1880s, Fort Worth civic leaders knew that a major industry was needed to replace the dwindling income from trail herds. For a major cattle-shipping center, meat-packing seemed to be a logical venture. In 1890, thirty Fort Worth residents invested $10,000 each to help found the Fort Worth Dressed Meat and Packing Company, capitalized at $500,000. During the next few years, the company went through various managements. The nation's leading meat firms, Swift & Co. and Armour & Co., became interested in Fort Worth as a location in 1901. In an eleventh-hour action, Fort Worth succeeded in raising a $100,000 bonus to secure the plants. By 1909, Swift & Company and Armour were processing 1,200,000 cattle and 870,000 hogs annually. The plants were instrumental in Fort Worth's leap from a population of 26,688 in 1900 to 73,312 in 1910.

There were other benefits for a railroad center. In 1905, President Theodore Roosevelt visited. An estimated 20,000 persons greeted him at the T&P station and thousands more lined the streets. A roof collapsed under the weight of fifty spectators, but no one was injured. Roosevelt went to Oklahoma Territory on a wolf hunt with Burk Burnett and Tom Waggoner, two North Texas cattlemen who maintained homes in Fort Worth. Roosevelt again visited Fort Worth in 1911.

Yet, despite the number of physical improvements, the principal changes in Fort Worth in the decades at the turn of the century were focused on the quality of life. Time confirmed Paddock's thesis that "social pleasures increase and multiply as refinement ploughs its way into rugged western life."

In those years the pace of living arrived at what J. Frank Dobie later would term "the right tempo." Not only was there an abundance of rewarding entertainment and cultural diversion, but daily routines allowed sufficient time for discussion, savoring and reflection.

The variety of outlets available for leisure hours and the extent of the city's involvement reveal the tenor of the era. For instance, when the "pyrotechnic drama" *The Last Days of Pompeii* arrived in Fort Worth on October 18, 1890, more than 7,000 of the town's 23,076 residents "participated in games in vogue at the dawn of the Christian era" and witnessed a fireworks display intended to rival that of Pompeii's demise.

The nationwide Panic of 1893 was felt only slightly in Fort Worth's social life. Throughout the 1890s, the columns of the *Fort Worth Record* contained detailed accounts of church socials, lawn parties and elaborate dinners. The small rituals that enrich life became important. The gentleman who escorted the lady from the parlor to the dinner table was properly identified. Attention was devoted to decorations and table settings. Expense apparently was of no concern when guests were entertained in the growing number of baronial homes, such as those of Winfield Scott, Burk Burnett and Tom Waggoner.

Two military drill groups, the Fort Worth Fencibles and the Lloyd Rifles, provided both civic entertainment and a core of social life for members. The Fencibles were awarded the post of honor in the inaugural ceremonies of President-elect Grover Cleveland in 1893; the 45 men, 10 commissioned and noncommissioned officers and the special surgeon purchased new uniforms "to go in such style as will reflect credit not only on this city but the entire state." The two units volunteered for duty in the Spanish-American War, and were awaiting embarkation at Key West, Florida, when the Spanish government surrendered.

The wealth of cultural entertainment during the era was impressive by any standards. Various music clubs and social groups sponsored the appearances of many visiting artists. An average of one or more performers was offered each week throughout the season. They apparently were well received. For instance, when the Arion Club presented cellist Karl Smith on April 16, 1905, the *Fort Worth Record* noted that the musician "charmed the audience with his graceful and artistic playing, leaving many admirers behind him. Fort Worth's appreciation of the classics was demonstrated in the storm of applause that greeted each number on the programme, each number being so enthusiastically applauded as to require two encore numbers."

Fort Worth Opera House at Third and Rusk Streets (Commerce), first opened in 1883, evolved into Greenwall's Opera House in 1900, and became the city's center of culture and entertainment. *The Mikado, The Toreador, The Burgermaster, East Lynne* and similar standards were offered, but the range of material was wide. The famous Lew Dockstader Minstrels visited, as did a dramatization of the comic strip, *Happy Hooligan.* Kirk La Shell's stage production of Owen Wister's novel, *The Virginian,* opened at Greenwall's on December 18, 1904. The *Fort Worth Record's* reviewer "found no flaw" in the portrayal of the Virginian by a young actor, Dustin Farnum, still a decade away from Hollywood and fame in *The Squaw Man.* Noting that few Western or Southern plays are favorably received in the lands they are supposed to represent, the reviewer termed *The Virginian* "a splendid dramatization of the novel; the very heart of the book is presented and nothing of any consequence is lost. The cowboys were cowboys; they did not play at being cowboys." And lest anyone assume that the reviewer made his judgment from a narrow context, let it be noted that on the night after *The Virginian* closed, Joseph De Crasse opened in productions of *The Merchant of Venice* and *Hamlet*. Among thespians who performed in the opera house were Lilly Langtry, Elenora Duse, Edwin Booth, Lillian Russell, Harry Lauder, Sarah Bernhardt, Douglas Fairbanks, and John, Ethel and Lionel Barrymore.

The Mandolin Club, the Literary Society, theatrical groups and a number of military bands were evidence that many residents were not satisfied to limit themselves to roles of spectators in artistic pursuits. They also added to the city's cultural fare.

Paddock wrote of the era with nostalgia: "There were picnics in the daytime and by moonlight, when the moon was in commission. Everybody was happy and tried to make his neighbor happy. Good old days."

In the first decade of the new century, evidence grew that the quiet, serene "good years" were coming to a close.

NOTES, THE GOOD YEARS

32. The bell today is displayed in front of Central Fire Station.

33. Quanah Parker was the son of Cynthia Ann Parker, taken by the Comanches in 1836 at the age of 9. His father was Peta Nocona, a Comanche chief.

34. A monument to Al Hayne was erected at the intersection of Main and Lancaster Streets.

35. The Arlington Inn was located northwest of the intersection of today's Crestline Road and Merrick.

36. Fort Worth University, in a series of mergers, eventually became Oklahoma City University.

45. The latest of the three lithographic city views of Fort Worth was completed in 1891 by Henry Wellge and the American Publishing Company of Milwaukee. It was distributed in Fort Worth by the Fort Worth Land and Investment Company. Although the print is quite similar to the 1886 view, there have been some significant changes. The Spring Palace is pictured in the left center of the print, for example, even though it burned on May 30, 1890. Amon Carter Museum Collection.

46. Residence of Dr. and Mrs. Julian Theodore Feild, 706 West Belknap. Dr. Feild's family called him "Dr. Pappa." Courtesy Mrs. Joseph J. Minton, Fort Worth.

47. The home of Capt. B. B. Paddock in Fort Worth. His brother William can be seen near the front door. Courtesy Mrs. C. W. Hutchison and Mrs. Martha Pitner Cort, Fort Worth.

48. Home of Colonel Richard M. Wynne, 1000 West Weatherford, Fort Worth, about 1895. Amon Carter Museum Collection.

49. Colonel Richard Wynne at his ease in his comfortable parlor. A Fort Worth attorney, he was a gubernatorial candidate in 1898 and later served as superintendent of the Confederate Home for Men in Austin. Amon Carter Museum Collection.

50. The residence of Thomas Jennings, May 24, 1894.
Courtesy Fort Worth Public Library.

51. Main Street, Fort Worth, looking south from the courthouse. The Texas & Pacific Railroad Station can be seen at the end of the street. Amon Carter Museum Collection.

52. Photographer D. H. Swartz caught this view of the Tarrant County Courthouse while it was "domeless" and under construction. Built in 1894, the courthouse was one of the finest structures of its kind in the state, and, today, is one of the best extant examples of nineteenth century courthouses remaining. Courtesy Fort Worth Public Library.

53. Tarrant County Courthouse soon after completion.
Courtesy W. D. Smith, Fort Worth.

54. A creative photographer captured this view of the Tarrant County Courthouse from Wire Bridge, northwest of the courthouse, in December, 1896. Courtesy Fort Worth Public Library.

55. Old settlers and the dates they came to Fort Worth: (top row, left to right): Howard W. Peak (1856), Captain J. C. Terrell (1857), Dan Parker (1858); (bottom row, left to right): Captain Sam Woody (1850), Captain Ed Terrell (1843), Richard King (1854). Photograph by C. L. Swartz, Fort Worth. Courtesy Fort Worth Public Library.

56. Old Fiddler's contest, Fort Worth, April 13, 1901.
Courtesy Fort Worth Museum of Science and History.

57. Street cars had been around for several years by the time this December, 1896, photograph was taken, although horses were still the main method of transportation. The recently completed courthouse dominates the scene from the north end of Main Street. Courtesy Fort Worth Public Library.

58. An early view of the Fort Worth Stockyards. Apparently these fellows are participating in a stock competition. Courtesy Fort Worth Museum of Science and History.

59. The famous Comanche chief, Quanah Parker, frequently visited Fort Worth, both on business and for the Fat Stock Show. He is pictured in the center on the white horse during an appearance at the stock show in March, 1909, held in the North Side Coliseum. The *Fort Worth Record* noted that a band of 38 full-blooded Comanche and Kiowa Indians accompanied him. Burk Burnett is shown at the extreme left. Courtesy Mrs. Charles Tandy, Fort Worth.

60. Early view of Fort Worth stockyards and packing plants.
Courtesy Norman Bradford, Fort Worth.

61. Taken at the inaugural run of the Fort Worth-Dallas Interurban, about 1907.
Shown are officials of the Fort Worth Traction Company and Stone and Webster.
Courtesy Sam B. Cantey III, Fort Worth.

62. Officials of the Fort Worth Traction Company and Stone and Webster celebrate the inaugural run of the Fort Worth-Dallas Interurban with a barbecue. 1907. Courtesy Sam B. Cantey III, Fort Worth.

63. This trolley took citizens from the courthouse to Lakeview and back prior to 1909. Even then, real estate agents were eager to develop the suburbs. Amon Carter Museum Collection.

64. Surrey driven by an officer of the Fort Worth Fencibles about 1895.
Courtesy Fort Worth Public Library.

65. Some of the popular sporting fashions of the day are shown in this picture, taken at an outing at Hurst Lake about 1907. Created in the summer of 1887, Hurst Lake was first known as Hirsch Lake, and the incorporating body was the Hirsch Lake Art Club. Apparently the name was soon changed to "Hurst Lake." An item in the *Fort Worth Democrat* of September 29, 1887, noted that "workmen will begin this morning on a new clubhouse at Hurst Lake. It will be 30 by 60 feet, and with broad verandas all around." Seated, second from right, Mrs. Julian T. Feild. Standing, left to right: Dr. W. A. Duringer, Mrs. Duringer, unknown, Dr. Julian Theodore Feild. Courtesy Mrs. Joseph J. Minton, Fort Worth.

66. This group of men was attending an outing of some sort — a picnic, races, etc. Well-known newspaperman Captain B. B. Paddock is shown seated in the left center of the picture in the light hat. Courtesy Mrs. C. W. Hutchison and Mrs. Martha Pitner Cort, Fort Worth.

67. Both men and women enjoyed one of the most popular sports of the day, hunting plover. Courtesy *Fort Worth Star-Telegram*.

68. This relaxing scene took place at an outing party for Miss Stella Root at the Hurst Lake Art Club in April, 1899. The photographer was Charles L. Swartz of Fort Worth. Courtesy Fort Worth Public Library.

69. These Fort Worth residents were having a fling in front of the boat house and gazebo at Hurst Lake. Courtesy Fort Worth Public Library.

70. Members of the Fort Worth Club in 1896. John Burke is seated beside the snowman. Back row, left to right: Nat Stubbs, Jim Davis, H. Hunter, Mullett, unknown, Stuart Moore, Diltz, Van Zandt, Tom Johnson, Jim Riley, A. P. Nicholson, Clapp. Courtesy First National Bank.

71. One of the long-standing and most popular pastimes for residents of Fort Worth was an afternoon spent watching the legendary Fort Worth Cats baseball team. The Cats franchise later merged with the Dallas franchise to become the Dallas-Fort Worth Spurs, which gave way to the present Texas Rangers. This photograph, probably taken in the early 1890s, shows one of the early Cats teams. Courtesy Fort Worth Public Library.

72. An early Fort Worth band. Courtesy *Fort Worth Star-Telegram*.

73. One of the more popular features of the Fort Worth Mandolin Club was the Waldo Quintette, made up of, seated, left to right: unknown, Hatcher James, John "Blinkie" Trimble, standing: Thomas P. Marlin, and Malcolm Moore. Courtesy Fort Worth Public Library.

74. Conrad Rhau was a popular music teacher in Fort Worth in 1885 and 1886. Mary Feild recalled that he was her first music teacher. Courtesy Fort Worth Public Library.

75. The Fort Worth Opera House was one of the main entertainment attractions of the city when this photograph was taken in 1885. Cora Hogsett, a Fort Worth teen-ager then, noted in her diary on January 15, "Last night we went to the theatre. The play was 'The Silver King' and was splendid." Courtesy Fort Worth Public Library.

76. One of the most popular recreation spots at the turn of the century was the Lake Como Casino. This picture probably was taken about 1910. Courtesy Fort Worth Public Library.

77. Lake Erie was one of the favorite sites of Fort Worth residents for a Sunday afternoon stroll. The power plant in the background did not diminish the enjoyment of this afternoon walk. Courtesy Fort Worth Public Library.

78. Old Fort Worth High School, built at Jennings and Daggett at a cost of $125,000. It was destroyed by fire in 1910. Courtesy W. D. Smith, Fort Worth.

79. Only a few people attended this school in Arlington Heights when this photograph was taken around 1905. Courtesy Mrs. T. E. D. Hackney, Fort Worth.

80. Founded in 1881 as Texas Wesleyan University (not to be confused with the present Texas Wesleyan College), Fort Worth University opened in downtown quarters, but soon moved to the site pictured here on College Avenue. A law school was added in 1893 and a medical school was established the following year. In its prime, the university occupied a ten-acre campus with enough space for baseball, football, croquet, lawn tennis, and other sports. The four main buildings, shown left to right, Cadet Hall, Science Hall, Gymnasium, and Administration Building, are shown on the 1886 and 1891 bird's eye views of the city. Fort Worth University left the city after Texas Christian University was established here in 1910, and, through a series of mergers, became what is today Oklahoma City University. Courtesy Mrs. Catherine Terrell McCartney, Fort Worth.

81. Botany Class, Fort Worth University, 1892. Left to right: Plenny Fosdick, James Daniel Easley, Thomas R. White, Clifton Humphreys, Fred Neye, Mr. Martin (the science teacher), unknown, Josie Terrell, unknown, Annie Tandy, unknown, and Mary Lou Trimbel. Courtesy Fort Worth Public Library.

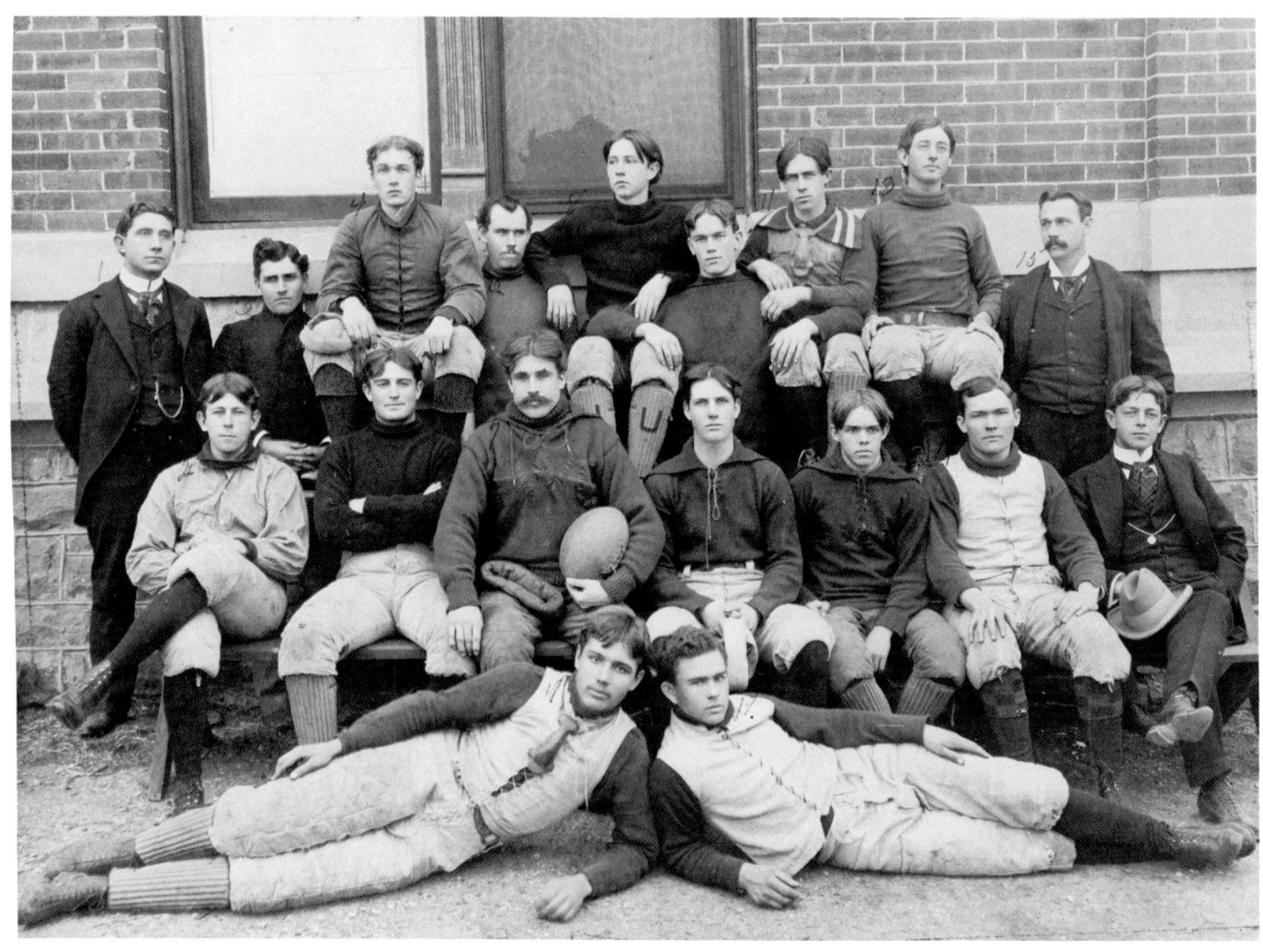

82. Football team, Fort Worth University, 1896. Among those identified are: (1) Mr. Morton, (5) A. T. Newman, (10) Elmore Tankersley, (11) W. J. Doyle, (12) William Bateman, (15) Dr. Kent Kibbie, and (7) Charles Wilburn Leigh, the coach, in the center. Courtesy Mrs. W. H. Portwood, Fort Worth.

83. The Literary Society of Fort Worth University, 1891. (1) Thomas R. White, (2) Richardson, (3) James Daniel Easley, (4) Wiley, (5) John J. Terrell, (7) Wing, (12) J. E. Edgington, (14) John Cox, (15) Fred Neye. Courtesy Fort Worth Public Library.

84. Fort Worth apparently earned its western reputation legitimately, as these girls of the Wild West Club of Polytechnic College demonstrate. From *The Panther City Parrot* (Polytechnic, Texas: Polytechnic College, 1906).

85. Founded in 1873 at Thorp Springs, Texas Christian University first moved to Waco, then to Fort Worth in 1910. This photograph, taken about 1913, is one of the earliest known of the campus in southwest Fort Worth. Amon Carter Museum Collection.

86. One of the more imaginative parties of the November, 1899, season must have been this Japanese Reception at Ella Hogsett's. Attending the party were: Ella Hogsett, Donnie Lee Carter, Mary Waller, Annie Samuels, Florence Adams, Grace Potter of Gainesville, Frances Tarlton, Ann Fields, Jennie Walker Davis, Ora Stroud Slack, Abbie Johnston, Grace Gant Hollingsworth, Susie Bell Beaumont, May Bell Bradley, Lola Binyon, Maisie Bewley, Alberta Griffith, Tommie Montgomery, Louise Orrick Binyon, and Anna Hogsett Ballard. The photographer who captured this unique picture was Charles L. Swartz. Courtesy Fort Worth Public Library.

87. "We had been to a card party. Afterwards on our way home, we decided to have our picture taken," is penciled on the reverse of the photograph. About 1896. Courtesy Mrs. Laura Hogsett Portwood, Fort Worth.

88. A strong esprit de corps was developed during the Civil War. Confederate veterans became lifelong friends and continued to hold reunions well into the 20th century. Their wives and families joined them on these special occasions. Courtesy Fort Worth Public Library.

89. The Flower Parade and Festival as it proceeded down Main Street toward the Texas & Pacific Railroad Station in May, 1900. Courtesy Fort Worth Public Library.

90. These cheerful girls were also ready to ride in Fort Worth's Flower Parade. Courtesy *Fort Worth Star-Telegram*.

91. Riding in this decorated buggy in the Flower Parade are (left to right): Mary Feild of Denison, Eva Edrington, unknown, and Willie Feild. Mary is standing at right. Courtesy Mrs. Joseph J. Minton.

92. Mary Feild of Fort Worth, Mary Feild of Denison, Willie Feild, and Eva Edrington ride in the Flower Parade. A notation on the back of the picture reads, "We won a blue ribbon." Courtesy Mrs. Joseph J. Minton.

93. In 1889, citizens of Fort Worth began construction of the Texas Spring Palace, a major trade fair to be held in Fort Worth. Colorful lithographic posters of the Spring Palace were issued as advertisements. They were pasted on walls and used as billboards. On very fragile paper, few of them have lasted until today. Courtesy Mrs. C. W. Hutchison, Fort Worth.

94. The Texas Spring Palace was under construction in June, 1889, when this photograph was taken. All products of the "field, forest, orchard and garden" were displayed in the various county and city booths. This detail of the Palace shows the McLennan County section. Photograph by Rhine, corner of Fourth and Main. Courtesy Fort Worth Museum of Science and History.

95. Literally thousands of people visited the Spring Palace during the short time that it was open. These sightseers are obviously enjoying the panorama from their second story perch. Courtesy *Fort Worth Star-Telegram*.

96. The Texas Spring Palace was a unique construction, built in honor of the produce of the state. Shown on the 1891 "bird's eye view" of the city, it was located west of the Texas & Pacific Railroad station. Built completely of materials produced in Texas, the Spring Palace received national attention when it was completed in 1889. Courtesy Mrs. C. W. Hutchison and Mrs. Martha Pitner Cort, Fort Worth.

97. When the Texas Spring Palace was destroyed by flames on May 30, 1890, the special railroad car for *Frank Leslie's Illustrated Newspaper,* the Mayflower, was on the Texas & Pacific tracks directly opposite the inferno. George E. Burr, the chief artist, was awakened and went out on the platform of the car to make the sketch from which this woodcut was taken. The reporter for Leslie's wrote: "No incident in the recent history of Texas has been more startling than the destruction by fire of the famous Texas Spring Palace at Fort Worth, on the night of Decoration Day. The palace was about to be closed, and the great event commemorating the successful Exposition of the year was to have been a grand full-dress ball. Visitors were present, including ladies representing the best families, from all parts of the state.

"A boy stepped on a match near the base of a decorated column, and the tiny spark thus created... enveloped the entire upper floor in less than a hundred seconds...."

A. S. Hayne, who helped rescue many people from the fire, died in the effort. A monument was later erected to him on the spot at Houston and East Lancaster streets and still stands today. Courtesy Library Company of Philadelphia.

98. Fort Worth's old Flatiron Building, copied after its more famous namesake in New York City, was built in 1908. Courtesy Fort Worth Public Library.

99. Graham Brothers Grocery Store, Fort Worth.
Amon Carter Museum Collection.

100. Law office of William Capps and Sam B. Cantey. Fort Worth. 1890s.
Courtesy Sam B. Cantey III, Fort Worth.

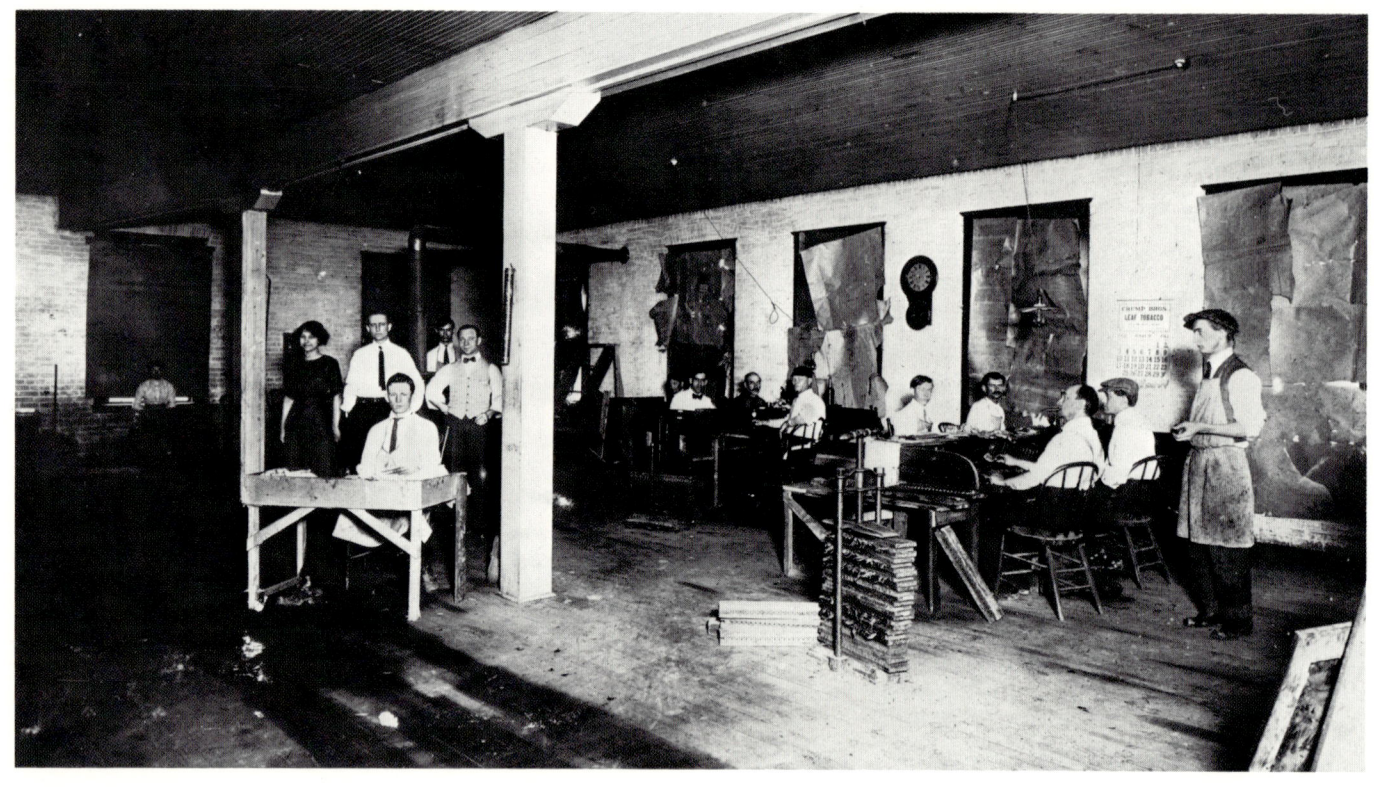

101. The Westland Cigar Manufacturing Company, located at 209½ West 11th Street, sold Blue Bells for five cents each and Westlands Bests at 15 cents, both made in Fort Worth. Shown is the interior of the company in 1912. Courtesy Fort Worth Public Library.

102. Officers and staff of First National Bank, Fort Worth. Left to right: J. M. Tenmey, L. C. Mayes, Thomas Winston, S. D. Triplett, H. T. Gahagan, R. C. Martin, T. W. Slack, W. E. Connell, M. B. Loyd, president of the bank, W. P. Andrew, Dallas Massay, and Greene Loyd. Courtesy First National Bank, Fort Worth.

103. The Famous Shoe Store, 709 Houston Street, carried one of the most complete stocks of footwear in town. It was also known as Fort Worth's oldest shoe store in 1912. Courtesy Fort Worth Public Library.

V. THE AWAKENING

104. Amon Carter, Sr. as a young man, left, with a friend.
Amon Carter Museum Collection.

More than 15,000 Fort Worth residents filled the Driving Park between West Seventh Street and White Settlement Road on January 12, 1911, to witness a new marvel—the flying machine.[37] The occasion was auspicious beyond the recording of Fort Worth's first airplane flight. Among those instrumental in bringing the seven daredevil pilots to Fort Worth was Amon G. Carter, whose major role in the city's long association with aviation was to typify the profound influence he was to have on Fort Worth.

Carter and other flying enthusiasts raised $5,000 to lure to Fort Worth a group of pilots billed as "International Aviators." The aviators had just participated in the first international air show in Belmont Park, New York. They were touring the country, performing aerial exhibitions. Their flimsy planes were transported by rail. John B. Moisant, one of the original group, had been killed in a performance at New Orleans.

The Fort Worth crowd grew restless that day while the aviators kept tinkering with their machines. Word was passed that the wind was too strong. The crowd patiently waited four more hours while the aviators sent up various kites to test air currents. Eventually, an initial effort was made. The *Fort Worth Star-Telegram* reported the results:

> The first actual thrill of the afternoon came when Edmond Audemars in his little yellow Demoiselle leaped into the air, even though the Swiss aviator could not control the little trick machine in the cross currents of air that swept to and fro near the earth. The sputtering of the Demoiselle's engine made the crowd forget its long wait, and there was a buzzing expectancy of seeing for the first time a heavier than air machine leave the ground. The Demoiselle skipped swiftly across the field, and as it neared the judge's stand it made a jerky leap into the air. Audemars' flights, however, were unsuccessful Thursday, and the best exhibition that the Demoiselle could furnish was a series of "hops."

The aviators were aware that the crowd was becoming disappointed and lapsing back into its former restlessness.

"I'm not going to see them disappointed," said Roland Garros, the French aviator, who only two hours before had shaken his head significantly and commented to his fellow birdmen on the peril of attempting a flight in the puffy wind that he knew was in the air.

Rene Simon, the "fool flyer" himself, grasped Garros by the arm almost in fright, and told him he must not try to fly at the risk of his life. Simon and the other aviators were still pleading with Garros when the mechanicians started the engine of the "Statue of Liberty" monoplane and Garros mounted the machine.

To the crowd that already had seen the failure of the Demoiselle, the whirr of Garros' high-power engine gave no unusual thrills. It expected more "hopping." When the engine had attained its highest speed, Garros raised his left hand, the mechanicians released the machine and it sped smoothly across the field.

When it mounted gracefully into the air and moved steadily upward for several hundred feet, the crowd burst into applause. Every head bent upward and not an eye left the machine until it curved gracefully to the left, soared above the grand stand and flew rapidly northward. So high was the monoplane when it passed over the heads of the spectators that the terrific throbbing of its powerful engine could be heard only as a murmur.

Farther into the distance the machine flew and persons on every side were heard explaining to others that Garros was lost, that he already had lost his directions. The bird-like contour of the aeroplane became a blur against the sky and the spectators watched intently at the marvel.

It was when the monoplane turned backward and sped toward the aviation field that thousands of people realized the peril of Garros. As the machine neared the field it could be seen rocking in the gusts of wind, and when it swerved almost to turn topsy-turvy the crowd held its breath. Before Garros reached the grounds of the Driver's Club, he pointed the nose of his machine downward and it looked as if he would plunge into the crowd at the north end of the track. The machine held its poise, however, became steadier, and the daring Frenchman alighted gracefully in almost the exact spot where the rubber-tired wheels of his machine had left the earth.

The crowd was wild and the big police squad patrolling the track could not stay the rush that started for the infield. Garros' fellow aviators were most enthusiastic. They seized his hands when he alighted from his seat and congratulated him on his return to safety and on his courage that made him risk his life to satisfy the crowd.[38]

"Fool Flyer" Rene Simon thrilled a crowd of 10,000 persons the next day with another flight. Audemars' Demoiselle was seriously damaged in its second effort to perform. The pilots received $6,300 for the two-day visit.

There had been rumblings of a new age even before the International Aviators or Amon Carter came to Fort Worth.

The first horseless carriage arrived in 1902 or 1903.[39] First regarded as curiosities, the automobiles soon came to be looked upon by many as nuisances. On May 20, 1904, the City Council passed an ordinance requiring registration, and decreed that each car must have two lights visible for a quarter of a mile at night, and that drivers must sound a gong or honk a horn audible for at least six hundred feet. The motorist was required to sound his device one hundred feet before each intersection and continue to do so until he was safely past. The speed limit was set at ten miles per hour.

There was some evidence that the horseless carriages might be of some worth. On August 24, 1903, Colonel R. Peterson of Paris, Texas, traveled from Dallas to Fort Worth in one hour and thirty-five minutes. By 1909, heavy-footed motorists became so numerous that the city added a motorcycle officer to the police department. Henry Lewis, at 19, corralled speeders from his five-horsepower Indian motorcycle.[40] The fire chief was outfitted in 1909 with a Maxwell passenger car. A fire extinguisher was mounted on the left runningboard, and a spotlight was installed in the place of a windshield. Two fire trucks were added six months later. But most early car owners were of the same mind as Emory T. Ambler, who after acquiring his Rambler about 1909 kept his horses for two more years, not entirely trusting the new machine.

If anyone missed the significance of the first airplane flight in Fort Worth, he was given an even stronger clue to the new age on October 17, 1911, when an airplane arrived in town under its own power.

Calbraith Perry Rodgers was on a transcontinental flight sponsored by a soft drink called Vin-Fiz. As he flew from town to town, his family and aides rode a special train. His leap-frog trip from New York had required more than a month.

An estimated 10,000 people gathered in the Ryan pasture[41] for Rodgers' arrival. When he left Denison at 9:25 a.m., a *Star-Telegram* correspondent wired that the flier was on the way. At Whitesboro, Rodgers followed the wrong railroad tracks out of town. Telegraph and telephone operators along the route were asked to signal him. Rodgers got the message at Bonita, and turned toward Fort Worth.

Rodgers' plane was sighted by the Fort Worth crowd shortly after 3 p.m. It first appeared as a speck far to the northwest. As the plane approached, the excitement became so great that the police could not handle the crowd. Thousands swarmed onto the field where Rodgers was to land.

Rodgers recognized his difficulty and quickly arrived at a solution. He pretended to be setting his plane down on one edge of the field. As the crowd rushed in that direction, he soared overhead and landed on the opposite side.

Among those who greeted Rodgers as he stepped from his plane was Amon G. Carter. The youngest Chamber of Commerce president in Fort Worth's history, Carter was perfecting his own brand of civic promotion.[42]

Born in an unchinked log cabin at Crafton, Wise County, on December 11, 1879, Carter had worked hard since his early years. His mother died in 1892, when he was 13. His father married a woman with three children and settled in Sunset. Carter left the crowded home and walked to Bowie. In the Horatio Alger tradition he established a reputation for frugality, enterprise and salesmanship. He worked for a time in the boarding house of Mrs. Mollie Jarrott as waiter and male "chamber maid" for $1.50 a week. He sold chicken sandwiches to passengers traveling on the Fort Worth & Denver City Railroad, which had no dining car. Several other boys shared in that business venture. When hens could not be found for the right price, rabbit meat occasionally was substituted.

In the 1890s, Carter went to Norman, Oklahoma, where for a time he worked in a confectionery. The hours were long, the pay low, and the job confining. Carter soon found work more to his liking, as a salesman for a portrait firm. The portraits, of an odd size, were given free under an arrangement with local merchants. The firm also supplied frames that would fit the portraits. The price of the frame more than offset the cost of the free portrait.

Carter traveled throughout the United States for the firm. He left the company as general sales manager. He then worked for a time with an advertising agency in San Francisco.

Carter was aware that Fort Worth had doubled in population in a few short years after the arrival of the meat packing and processing plants. He had always held Fort Worth in high esteem as "*the* city" while living in Bowie. He decided to return to Fort Worth and to share in the town's rapid growth.

In 1905, he established a one-man firm, the Texas Advertising and Manufacturing Company. The principal products were a patented indexing telephone directory and advertising cards for streetcars.

Later that year, he joined with Louis J. Wortham in founding the *Fort Worth Star* to compete with the existing *Fort Worth Telegram.* Through lean times, Carter, Wortham, J. M. North, Jr., B. N. Honea and James R. Record guided the *Star* to that milestone of 1908 when it bought out the rival *Telegram.*

Carter's exceptional energies and talents found even greater expression with the *Star-Telegram.* The many facets of his character were revealed. In the early years, he served as the newspaper's advertising and business manager, frequently preserving the firm from bankruptcy. Yet, he possessed an innate "news sense" and functioned well in the editorial department. When word of the San Francisco earthquake came on a stockbroker's wire, Carter achieved a complete regional scoop by blending the few available details with his own knowledge of San Francisco. Business promotion, civic need and unabashed personal empathy were effectively combined in such programs as a "milk and ice fund" for the indigent, a Goodfellows Fund to provide "toys and goodies" for poor children at Christmas, and "outings" for orphans. Editorially, the newspaper identified itself with "practical city building" through the formation of an industrial investment company to attract industry and business to Fort Worth.

Carter's leadership was quickly recognized. He was one of the founders of the Fort Worth Advertising Club. As Exalted Ruler of the Fort Worth Elks Club, he led the campaign to build a new clubhouse.

As early as 1911, the *Star-Telegram* printed almost daily news of events pointing toward war in Europe. Yet, even when war broke out in Europe in 1914, the trouble seemed remote to most Americans. Carter and the other leaders of Fort Worth perhaps were awakened to America's impending involvement sooner than most of the nation. Their awareness was to contribute greatly to Fort Worth's extensive role in World War I.

An unusual visitor to Fort Worth introduced the grim realities of the nation's plight. Fort Worth civic leaders were hosts on November 20, 1915, to the entire U.S. air force. The group fitted comfortably into a private dining room at the Metropolitan Hotel. The aero squadron, the Army's first, was en route from Fort Sill, Oklahoma, to San Antonio to establish permanent headquarters at Fort Sam Houston. More than 10,000 residents witnessed the arrival of the squadron's seven planes as they landed in Ryan's pasture. In command of the squadron was a tall, imposing, strikingly handsome young Army captain, Benjamin D. Foulois, who had gained some fame as the military's first pilot. After logging 15 minutes of flying time with the Wright brothers, Foulois had been put in charge of the Army's first airplane when it was purchased in 1910.

During the lengthy, relaxed dinner at the Metropolitan, Captain Foulois astonished his hosts by predicting that in case of war, the government immediately would be required to spend $100,000,000 for the development of air power.[43]

He further surprised the group by predicting that America's next war would be with Germany. Some disagreement was voiced. Captain Foulois gave the group his reasons for concern: "If Germany comes out victorious in this war, she will have the strongest army in the world . . . . If Germany cared to take issue with the United States after this European war, she could land troops anywhere she pleased along the Atlantic coast and take every munition factory we have—they are all along the Atlantic coast."

Captain Foulois warned that the nation was in poor shape, militarily. "Our little army today would be wiped out in the first good fight we had," he said. "We wouldn't be ready to fight if war were declared now. We wouldn't be ready in a year. Nor would we be ready in five years if our condition were no better than it is today."

Captain Foulois urged the businessmen to appeal to their congressmen and demand that something be done. "The highest number of any one of the aeroplanes out yonder on the field tonight is 53," he said. "It means that many aeroplanes have been owned by the United States Army in the last six years. That many machines are being shipped to Europe every day. That many are being destroyed in Europe every day."

Foulois stressed the role of the airplane in European warfare, and the fact that America had only the bare beginnings of a flying corps.

"We have been trying for seven years to build our service up," he said. "It has been hard to do with no money and little encouragement. In 1910 I was sent to San Antonio with the only aeroplane in the service. I had to teach myself how to fly and the government allowed me $150 a year to keep the machine up. In the first year I spent $300 out of my own pocket on it. One of the speakers [tonight] has quoted a Texas congressman as having said 'preparedness' is all graft. I don't think you could have called me a grafter under such circumstances."[44]

Captain Foulois' argument proved prophetic. Within a year, there were three military fields near Fort Worth, training pilots for war. The Royal Flying Corps of Canada selected Fort Worth as the site for three fields named Taliaferro, Barron and Carruthers, forming a triangle around the city.[45] Many Americans enlisted in the Canadian military units before the United States entered the war and were assigned to Fort Worth for pilot training.

The most famous Canadian pilot assigned to Fort Worth was Captain Vernon Castle, of the husband-wife dancing team. One afternoon Captain Castle and five other officers drove to Waxahachie to visit friends. Their Rolls-Royce developed engine trouble. Judge O. E. Dunlap, a Waxahachie banker, invited the group to return to Fort Worth in his personal car. He suggested that his personal chauffeur, Ely Green, could return the Rolls when it was repaired.

As Green drove the group to Fort Worth in the judge's car, he queried Captain Castle about the possibilities of his enlisting for air training. Half white, half black, Ely Green had been a personal servant for Judge Dunlap for many years. As a chauffeur in the early days of automobiles, he had mastered the finer points of mechanics. Judge Dunlap often transferred considerable sums of money among his various enterprises. He often did not use guards, but depended on Green's talent for fast driving. Green told Castle that he had raced cars with Ormer Locklear, one of Castle's outstanding pilots.[46] Green gave Castle a list of his qualifications, and explained his theory that if he could get to France, he would gain fame as a black aviator and "win my rights as a citizen of the United States."

Captain Castle admitted that there were no blacks in the Royal Flying Corps. He apparently was moved by Green's plea. After a few thoughtful minutes, he said that there might be a way for Green to learn to fly. He suggested that Green could enlist in the U.S. Army, asking for a delay of ten days in reporting for duty. This delay, he explained, would give him time to ask for Green as his orderly. Captain Castle said he would teach Green to fly, and that by the time the squadron reached France, the concern would be not whether Green was black or white, but that he was an accomplished pilot.

Captain Castle told Green to wait a few days while he made certain that the plan was feasible.

Green found that the gas line strainer in Captain Castle's Rolls was clogged, and easily repaired. He returned the car to Castle the following day at the Westbrook Hotel in Fort Worth, where Castle and his wife Irene were in residence. Captain Castle said he had ascertained that the plan would work. He advised Green that upon completion of the enlistment, he should be notified immediately so he could request Green's transfer.

A week later Green drove to Fort Worth and enlisted. After completing the paper work, he drove toward Carruthers Field at Benbrook to notify Captain Castle. En route he met an ambulance. At the airfield gate, Green learned that Captain Castle's plane had just crashed on landing. To avoid a student pilot, Castle was forced to put his plane into a climb near the ground. The plane stalled and fell to earth. Captain Castle was killed. The ambulance Green had met was taking the captain's body to Fort Worth.

Green spent most of World War I with black stevedore gangs in the holds of ships, unloading material on the docks of France.

At least thirty-eight Canadian pilots were killed in training at Fort Worth's three fields.[47] Captain Castle's death was the fifty-first among pilots of all nationalities at the fields, and the fifth in a week. For a time, Taliaferro Field had the highest total of flying time and the greatest number of fatalities of all fields in the United States.

The early deaths were blamed on the fact that the pilots were taught conservative flying. Shallow banks and slow turns were considered proper. Sharp maneuvers were termed "stunting," and frowned upon. As a consequence, when a flier was faced with an unexpected situation, he often lacked the necessary skill to avert tragedy. This error in training philosophy was reversed abruptly to the other extreme as combat fliers began returning from France to supervise instruction. Both men and planes were pushed to their limitations. At least 106 deaths occurred at the three fields during all phases of training.

Shortly after the United States entered the war on April 6, 1917, command of the fields was assumed by the U.S. Army. The tempo of training was increased.

In June of 1917, an Army commission headed by a brigadier general arrived in Fort Worth to consider possible sites for a large training camp. In preparing for the visit, Fort Worth civic and business leaders assembled exhaustive material on two likely areas, one south of Southwestern Baptist Theological Seminary, and the other near Lake Worth. But on Main Street en route to the sites, the tour group happened to meet Colonel Holman Taylor, a veteran of the Mexican Expedition who was in Fort Worth recruiting Army doctors. When Colonel Taylor learned of the group's mission, he offered a suggestion.

"I know the best site in Texas for an Army camp," he said. "It's there in Arlington Heights, between the streetcar line and Stove Foundry Road."

Taylor explained that two years before, he had surveyed the area for a possible National Guard camp. He drove the general to the site. "Just look at that gravel surface, General," he said. "It just quit raining an hour ago and in a couple of hours more it will be dust here again."

Colonel Taylor's recommendation and Arlington Heights' graveled subsoil apparently proved convincing. After the general toured the other two potential sites, he returned to Arlington Heights to find that the tires of his car raised dust, just as Colonel Taylor had predicted. Fort Worth's civic and business leaders quickly shifted gears and extolled the area's other, less obvious virtues: close connections for spur railroads, an existing streetcar line, nearby lumber facilities, excellent utility services and a wealth of possible civilian employees. The general was persuaded.

In early July the announcement was made that Fort Worth would be the site of Camp Bowie, designed to house 35,000 men.

The camp seemed to spring into existence overnight. At one time 3,500 carpenters were at work. By December 1, the camp was ready. It contained acres of tents, barracks, rifle ranges, gas warfare instruction houses, 15 mess halls, a base hospital, an ammunition magazine, and a railroad spur to supply a row of warehouses.

The camp ranged from White Settlement Road to Stove Foundry Road, and from near the Seventh Street viaduct far to the west. The region from Lake Worth to Westover Hills served as the artillery range.

More than 100,000 men trained at Camp Bowie. For many, the stay in Fort Worth was marred by the restrictions of quarantine during the Spanish influenza epidemic. Although the men were allowed to visit town, they were forbidden to take part in any public gathering. Most of the social and entertainment programs planned for the soldiers were canceled. On October 23, 1918, the *Star-Telegram* reported: "Not a death occurred at Camp Bowie Base Hospital during the 24-hour period from noon Tuesday until noon Wednesday. It has been over a month since a similar report came from the hospital."

The war in Europe and local military activities now were competing for newspaper space with Fort Worth's next major impetus for growth—oil.

In October of 1917, a wildcat well on the John McCleskey farm one mile south of Ranger in Eastland County came in, gushing two-thirds of the height of the derrick. The discovery set off activity throughout West Texas. In July of 1918, a test well on the S. L. Fowler farm at Burkburnett in Wichita County was brought in, quickly filling a 1,200-barrel storage tank, and overflowing into the rows of Fowler's cotton patch. Within a month, more than a hundred wells were being drilled within the city limits. In September of 1918, a well on the Joe Duke farm near Desdemona, 18 miles south of Ranger, proved to be a gusher, caught fire, and burned out of control for two days. Desdemona, previously known to some as Hogtown, boomed from fifty residents to more than 16,000 within months. There were spectacular discovery wells at Eastland, Cisco, Breckenridge and various other West Texas locations during the next few years.

Fort Worth, long the headquarters for the cattle industry throughout West Texas, naturally became the center for the far-ranging oil speculation. During the last few months before the Armistice on November 11, 1918, the *Fort Worth Star-Telegram* daily devoted at least one page in each edition to reports from staff members and correspondents on the scene of oil activities throughout Texas and Oklahoma. The management of Fort Worth's Westbrook Hotel removed the furniture from the lobby to make room for the impromptu oil trading. The oil industry brought pressure on the state government for better roads throughout the region, and Fort Worth's ties to West Texas were strengthened.

The wartime economic and population growth of Fort Worth was blended smoothly and without pause into the postwar oil boom. In 1920, the U. S. census counted 106,472 Fort Worth residents—almost four times the 26,688 of only twenty years earlier.

This rapid growth brought lasting changes to Fort Worth's way of life. Oil, aviation, and the other new industries with which Fort Worth became preoccupied were attuned to a quicker tempo. The challenges of the era required leaders who were in league with the future.

Editor B. B. Paddock once lamented the journalistic necessity of citing various individuals for acclaim in civic efforts. He insisted that "with only one or two notable exceptions," the entire tax rolls could be accorded recognition. He said that virtually every resident had contributed to municipal development, each in keeping with his ability and in his own way.

In this context, Amon G. Carter, while outstanding, was perhaps also symbolic of a new generation of leaders who were to guide Fort Worth through the next few decades. He was remarkable because he was the most adroit practitioner of the talents demanded by the new era—indefatigable energy, persistent business acumen, a flair for showmanship, deep regional concern, and innate global attitudes. Yet, his personal philosophy clearly was a product of the frontier experience—a belief in the virtue of hard work, a deep appreciation of the individual, and a strong sense of self-identity.

Fort Worth's basic character was shaped in this mold of frontier experience, and tempered with the resolution of uncommon men.

Thus armed, Fort Worth was well prepared to meet the difficulties the next few decades would bring.

NOTES, THE AWAKENING

37. The old Driving Park was located just behind the present site of the Montgomery Ward building on West Seventh.

38. Roland Garros soon was to perform even greater feats. He was one of France's first combat aces in World War I.

39. The date is uncertain. H. R. Cromer, who sold Rambler bicycles, registered the first car, a Rambler, in 1903. Some local historians believe that minstrel man Billy Kasan purchased the first automobile in Fort Worth.

40. Henry Lewis later became police chief, holding that office from 1933 to 1937.

41. The Ryan pasture was in the later Ryan Place Addition, south of Elizabeth Boulevard.

42. In 1950, when a large number of Fort Worth citizens petitioned the Fort Worth City Council to designate the Fort Worth International Airport as Amon Carter Field, Marvin Leonard said, "Amon G. Carter brought the first aviation to Fort Worth and for forty years he has tirelessly and unselfishly devoted his boundless energy, and his own money, to the purpose of building here a great aviation center. His exceptional effort has brought to Fort Worth a cash flow of several billion dollars for payrolls, material and supplies, and it has brought more than twenty thousand happy and prosperous neighbors to our midst."

43. Captain Benjamin D. Foulois was conservative in his estimates. A few months later, Captain Foulois himself drafted the first aerial appropriations bill—for $640,000,000.

44. A half century later, Captain Foulois was still speaking his mind. At a Pentagon function in 1964, where he was honored as "the father of the Air Force," the 84-year-old retired general turned the affair into an impromptu political rally for presidential candidate Barry Goldwater.

45. After the United States entered World War I, the U. S. Army officially changed the names of the fields—Taliaferro to Hicks, Barron to Everman, and Carruthers to Benbrook. However, newspaper references were not consistent in observing the change.

46. Ormer Locklear, reared in Fort Worth, later became a performer in air shows and a Hollywood film star. He was the first pilot to change from one plane to another in mid-air. He was killed in a plane crash while filming *The Skywayman* in 1920. An estimated 50,000 people lined the streets of Fort Worth for his funeral procession.

47. Eleven Canadian fliers were buried in Fort Worth. For many years the location of their graves was lost. Just before World War II, the World War I Fliers Club began annual memorial services, honoring the pilots, at a monument erected at the gravesites in Greenwood Cemetery.

105. Composing room of the Fort Worth *Telegram*, 1904. The *Telegram* later was purchased by the Fort Worth *Star* and became the present *Star-Telegram*. Courtesy Fort Worth Public Library.

106. The Texas & Pacific Union Station was one of the primary landmarks in Fort Worth. This photograph was taken on the occasion of a visit of West Texans in 1902. The Hayne monument, erected by the Women's Humane Society in 1893, is seen at right center. Courtesy Fort Worth Public Library.

107. Texas & Pacific Railroad Station, before it was engulfed in fire prior to December, 1904. Courtesy Fort Worth Public Library.

108. President Theodore Roosevelt speaking in Fort Worth, April 8, 1905. Returning from a reunion with the Rough Riders in San Antonio, Roosevelt stopped to deliver a speech in front of the Missouri-Kansas-Texas Railroad Station, planted a tree in front of the public library, then continued to Oklahoma Territory. Amon Carter Museum Collection.

109. Residents of Fort Worth worked hard to decorate the city in preparation for President Roosevelt's visit. Amon Carter Museum Collection.

110. Roosevelt was the first President to visit Fort Worth when he arrived the morning of April 8, 1905. Amon Carter Museum Collection.

111. Streetcar track repair, looking north on Jennings Avenue. The low, dark building in the background is the Carnegie Public Library, replaced in the 1930s by the present library building. Courtesy W. D. Smith, Fort Worth.

112. Louis Bicocchi Grocery, the first store in Fort Worth with a cash register and electric lights. Courtesy Fort Worth Public Library.

113. J. L. Pummill's Meat Market and Delicatessen, located at 6 Jennings Avenue in 1912. W. L. French was the photographer. Courtesy Fort Worth Public Library.

114. Horses were still a necessity in 1912 and Nobby Harness Company, 600 Houston Street, kept the residents well supplied. The firm was open until recent years. Courtesy Fort Worth Public Library.

115. James A. Walkup invited all his friends to visit the "prettiest and most up-to-date Soda Fountain in the city" in 1912. It was located at the corner of Main and Fifteenth streets. Courtesy Fort Worth Public Library.

116. Interior of Graham Brothers Grocery Store. Amon Carter Museum Collection.

117. The Twentieth Street Drug Store called itself "the classy Northside store" in 1912. Courtesy Fort Worth Public Library.

118. This 1912 photograph of the Regan Millinery Shop shows the fashion selection available to Fort Worth ladies. Courtesy Fort Worth Public Library.

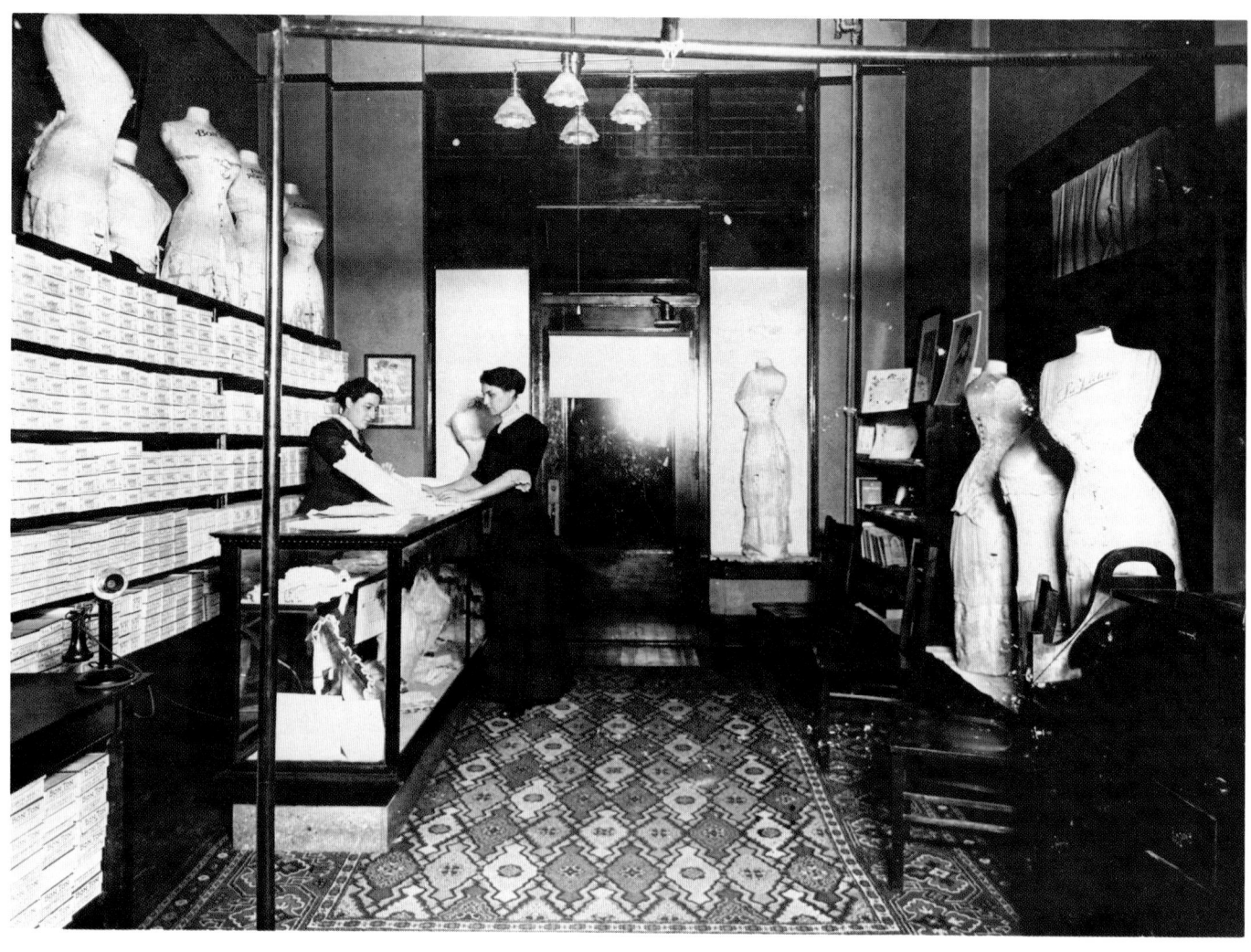

119. One of the important fashion shops in the city was Norvell Corset Shop, located in the Westbrook Hotel Building. "Exclusive Corsetieres, Fitting a Specialty," noted an advertisement in 1912. Courtesy Fort Worth Public Library.

120. Taken at the engagement party of Miss Floy Johnson (North) given by Mrs. E. E. Baldridge at her residence on the corner of Camp Bowie Boulevard and Sanguinet streets, 1913. Identified guests include Patti Allison, Frances Williamson, Gussie O'Keefe, Betty Reynolds, Jennie Ross, Floy Johnson, Mrs. Baldridge, Grace Ambler, Clay Allison, Lucy Stripling, May Taylor, Mrs. James North (mother of the groom-to-be), and Mrs. J. Lee Johnson (mother of the bride-to-be). Courtesy Sam B. Cantey III, Fort Worth.

121. The photographer caught Roland G. Garros preparing to take off in what became Fort Worth's first airplane flight in January, 1911. The flight was made at the old driving park behind what is now Montgomery Ward on Seventh Street. "Thursday's throng that was rewarded after four hours of patient waiting by the sight of the reckless Roland G. Garros rocking high above their heads was perhaps one of the largest ever gathered in Fort Worth," wrote one reporter. Courtesy *Fort Worth Star-Telegram.*

122. "Daredevil Cal" Rodgers landed the first plane to arrive in Fort Worth under its own power in the Ryan Pasture in August, 1911. Sponsored by a grape drink called Vin-Fiz, Rodgers piloted his "Vin-Fiz Flyer" from New York to Fort Worth in the first transcontinental flight in history. Courtesy *Fort Worth Star-Telegram.*

123. Emory T. Ambler with his chauffeur in a Rambler, 1226 Pennsylvania Avenue, about 1909. Courtesy Sam B. Cantey III, Fort Worth.

124. Children's Red Cross parade, June, 1917. Mrs. Joe B. Hogsett helps Sam B. Cantey III, Keating Chase, Jack Guthrie, and Bill Portwood. Courtesy Sam B. Cantey III, Fort Worth.

125. Captain Benjamin D. Foulois was commander of the air detachment that visited Fort Worth in 1915 under the sponsorship of Amon Carter. He was trained to fly by the Wright brothers and kept his U. S. military plane flying by meeting expenditures out of his own pocket. He was the first U. S. military pilot. Courtesy *Fort Worth Star-Telegram.*

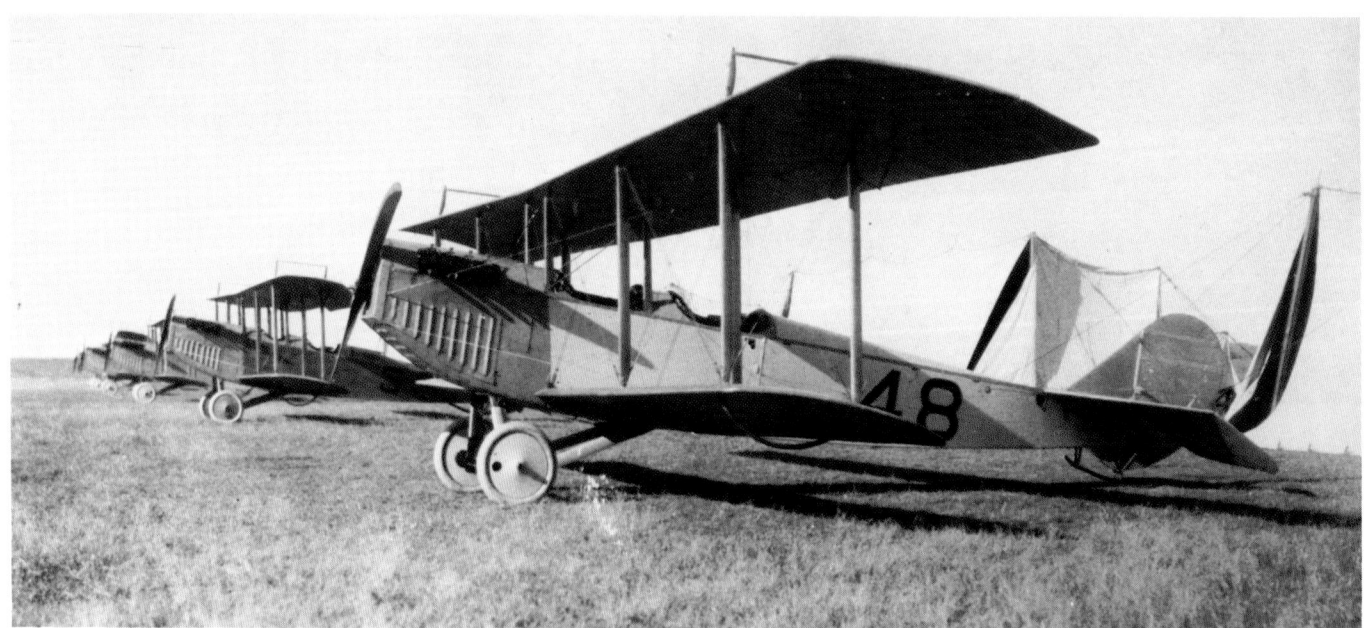

126. When the entire United States air force visited Fort Worth in 1915, the pilots were taken to dinner at the Metropolitan Hotel. All seven planes landed and were kept overnight at Ryan Pasture. Courtesy *Fort Worth Star-Telegram.*

127. The Canadian fliers being trained in Fort Worth during World War I found the Fort Worth girls delightful company. Courtesy Howard McPeak, Fort Worth.

128. Panorama of Camp Bowie during World War I.
Courtesy National Archives, Washington, D. C.

129. The 144th Infantry Regiment on a Sunday afternoon at Camp Bowie.
Courtesy National Archives, Washington, D. C.

130. Soldiers of the 144th Infantry Regiment relaxing at Camp Bowie.
Courtesy National Archives, Washington, D. C.

131. The street cars had difficulty plying their way through the traffic in this post-war parade scene looking north on Main Street. Courtesy Fort Worth Public Library.

NOTES ON SOURCES

Local history is an endeavor for the wary. Oral accounts and memoirs recorded long after the fact are suspect among professional historians. Recollections and oft-repeated stories frequently become sicklied o'er with human frailties. More bluntly: while a staggering amount of information is available on Fort Worth's early years, much misinformation also begs for attention. Considerable "documentation" exists, for instance, that Fort Worth was founded in 1848, not 1849. Yet, Army records, letters and other unimpeachable sources not only establish the year, but the exact day. Similar examples abound.

A local history by nature becomes a matter of choosing the "correct" information. For this reason, primary sources—Army records, nineteenth century records and newspapers, etc.—were consulted where possible. In many instances, the paths to the material have been blazed by others. For this, the author is extremely grateful.

Three books deserve special mention. Oliver Knight's *Fort Worth: Outpost on the Trinity,* now out of print and a collector's item, contains footnotes citing many of the valuable primary sources. Although flawed to some extent in basic organization and containing several errors of fact, the book is the most complete history extant on Fort Worth, and in addition merits respect as a pioneering effort. *Fort Worth: A Frontier Triumph* by Julia Kathryn Garrett is a wonderfully detailed account of the city's first 24 years. The book is gleaned from a wide variety of sources and contains an extensive bibliography. However, in most instances the exact origin of the text is not revealed. No book presents a better portrait of Fort Worth in its first decade; the site of each pioneer settler's home is pinpointed. K. M. Van Zandt's autobiography, *Force Without Fanfare,* is especially valuable in that it offers insights into the political and financial maneuverings behind Fort Worth's growth. The historical worth of Van Zandt's memoirs is enhanced immeasurably by the work of Dr. Sandra L. Myres, who painstakingly annotated the text, checking Van Zandt's recollections against primary sources. Supporting data for Van Zandt's memory are noted, and the few instances in which Van Zandt was in error are cited. No book offers a better sense of Fort Worth and North Texas at the close of the Civil War.

Following are specific sources for material in this volume, where not attributed in the text:

I. THE LEAN YEARS

Major Ripley A. Arnold and the Founding of Fort Worth: Orders of the Eighth Military Department and Reigstry of Returns thereof contain Major Arnold's assignment and his correspondence with his commanding officers. The papers of Brigadier General William S. Harney contain considerable material, including inspection reports and descriptions of the fort. Simon B. Ferrar's letter to C. C. Cummings, dated 1893, in the collection of Mrs. Catherine Terrell McCartney, describes Arnold's trip northward to select the site. Biographical data and background material on Arnold and General William J. Worth were derived chiefly from Theodore F. Rodenbough's *From Everglades to Canyon with the Second Dragoons; Chronicles of the Gringos* by George Winston Smith and Charles Judah, and Francis B. Heitman's *Historical Register and Dictionary of the United States Army.* Although Rodenbough does not mention Fort Worth's founding, he cites the exceptional record of both men in the Seminole War in Florida and in the Mexican War. *Chronicles of the Gringos,* compiled from diaries and letters written during the war, offers an unvarnished view of Worth, Arnold and the conditions in which they served.

The Indian Situation in North Texas in the 1840's: Texas Indian Papers, 1846-1859 contains considerable material, such as petitions from citizens of various counties to the governor, detailing Indian depredations and demanding that something be done about them. A letter from General Worth to Governor George Wood dated February 15, 1849, offers a candid view of the problem, and the general's plans toward a solution. J. W. Wilbarger's *Indian Depredations in Texas* provides a detailed chronological summary of horrors on the Texas frontier. In addition, most Texas newspapers of the time reprinted accounts from distant newspapers of Indian activities. Especially attuned to conditions in North Texas in the 1840s were the *Texas Sentinel* and *Daily Bulletin* in Austin, and the *Texas Republican* in Marshall.

Early Settlements in North Texas: The Englishman William Bollaert visited and wrote of Dallas and North Texas in 1844. His book, *William Bollaert's Texas,* describes the various settlements he encountered. Melinda Rankin's *Texas in 1850* provides a summary of the pattern of Texas settlement in that year. Wilbarger's *Indian Depredations in Texas* gives readers some idea of the location of the frontier at different times, and of the relationships of various settlements. Nineteenth century newspapers obviously considered reports of new settlements and frontier conditions choice material. Texas Writers Project, *Research Data, Fort Worth and Tarrant County,* Fort Worth Public Library, contains a wealth of material on local settlement. B. B. Paddock's *History and Biographical Record of North and West Texas* includes detailed accounts of the region's development.

Indian Confrontation at Fort Worth: Abe Harris, who was a sergeant-major of infantry, remained in Fort Worth at the termination of his enlistment, and described the event in many interviews. Paddock devoted most of a page to Harris' account in *History of North and West Texas.* Military records tend to support Harris' statement that the incident was the peaceful outcome of the only hostilities Fort Worth ever experienced. Heitman's *Historical Register and Dictionary of the United States Army* attributes no action to Fort Worth, nor is any incident mentioned in the fort returns. Only one mention hints of anything unusual: in April of 1851 Lt. Samuel H. Starr submitted information to General Harney that one Indian chief and five warriors were being held prisoner, and he asked what he should do with them.

Occupation of Abandoned Fort: Paddock's *History and Biographical Record of North and West Texas* lists the numerous residents who moved into various buildings. *Research Data* contains considerable material on the subject.

Fort Worth-Birdville Feud: Sam Woody's first-person account of the illegal voting is recorded in Paddock's *History of North and West Texas. Research Data* also contains much material on the subject. Wayne Gard's *Rawhide Texas* describes the shootings and cites sources. A chapter in Gard's book on violence among pioneer editors indicates that perhaps journalism, not law enforcement, was the most hazardous profession of the era.

Houston's Visits: The incident of Captain Eph Daggett and Santa Anna's silver washbowl is related in J. C. Terrell's *Reminiscences of the Early Days of Fort Worth. Research Data* also offers material. Both political campaigns are included in Marquis James' biography of Sam Houston, *The Raven,* which provides insight into the tenor of the time and Houston's response to the new demands made upon him.

Abolitionist Hangings: The *Texas State Gazette* in Austin and the *Dallas Herald* carried extensive reports of the uproar in Fort Worth. *Research Data* contains material. Paddock relates the events in *History of North and West Texas.*

Cynthia Ann Parker's Visit: J. W. Wilbarger's *Indian Depredations in Texas* describes the making of the famous daguerreotype of Cynthia Ann in Fort Worth. Incidentally, Quanah Parker advertised in a June, 1884, issue of the *Fort Worth Gazette,* seeking a copy of the picture.

II. THE BOOM YEARS

K. M. Van Zandt's Arrival: The observations and views of Van Zandt throughout this portion are derived chiefly from his autobiography, *Force Without Fanfare,* and quoted material in *Star-Telegram* interviews.

Captain Eph Daggett Cattle Drive: The Trail Drivers of Texas, edited by J. Marvin Hunter, contains Captain Daggett's description of the 1865 drive.

The Chisholm Trail: Wayne Gard's *The Chisholm Trail* remains the best source on the development and career of the northern cattle markets.

B. B. Paddock's Arrival: K. M. Van Zandt wrote in his autobiography of their meeting, as did B. B. Paddock in *Early Days in Fort Worth, Much of Which I Saw and Part of Which I Was.* Their accounts are virtually identical, with the exception that Van Zandt places Paddock's arrival a year later, in 1873.

Fort Worth in the Panic of 1873: Van Zandt's autobiography contains material, but perhaps Paddock is more colorful on the subject, especially in his earlier accounts.

Early Days in Fort Worth reveals Paddock in his best barbed eloquence. His later histories were more serious in tone.

Arrival of the Railroad: The details of the political and financial maneuvering are contained in Van Zandt's autobiography. Paddock's *Early Days in Fort Worth* describes the town's concertive effort, as does Vernon Gladden Spence in *Colonel Morgan Jones: Grand Old Man of Texas Railroading.*

The Boom Years: Van Zandt's autobiography, Paddock's *Early Days* and Paddock's *History and Biographical Record of North and West Texas* offer material on this era of rapid growth. Oliver Knight's *Fort Worth: Outpost on the Trinity* contains further details, and cites specific Fort Worth newspapers of the 1870s and 1880s as sources. Spence chronicles the growth of the railroad from the standpoint of its builder, Morgan Jones.

III. A BUNCH OF WILDNESS

Courtright's career in Fort Worth: The best biography of Fort Worth's most colorful gunman is F. Stanley's *Longhair Jim Courtright: Two Gun Marshal of Fort Worth.* Although flawed to some degree by Father Stanley's bias (Courtright ranks second only to Clay Allison in Father Stanley's admiration), the book is thoroughly researched and cites a wealth of primary sources. Jim McIntire's autobiography, *Early Days in Texas,* also is a valuable source in a study of Courtright. Their careers were entwined for several years. Eugene Cunningham's *Triggernometry* contains a section on Courtright, centered on his fatal gun battle with Luke Short. The only serious error noted in *Triggernometry* on the subject is Cunningham's location of the White Elephant Saloon. Apparently he accepted the information of "old-timers," who remembered the saloon in the 600 block of Main Street. The 1885-1886 City Directory leaves no doubt: at the time of the gun battle, the saloon was located at 308-310 Main Street, where it remained until the 1890s. All of the material on Courtright was put to the acid test of things western: Ramon F. Adams' *Burs Under the Saddle: A Second Look at Books and Histories of the Old West.*

Butch Cassidy and the Sundance Kid in Fort Worth: Information on the activities of the Wild Bunch in Fort Worth was obtained from James D. Horan's *The Wild Bunch* and *Pinkerton's, Inc.* Curiously, response from knowledgeable readers of Horan's earlier book, *Desperate Men,* unearthed the fact that the Wild Bunch hid out in Fort Worth. Following tips from former associates of the Wild Bunch, Horan set out on research that led him to the Pinkerton files and signed statements attesting to the gang's activities in Fort Worth. Delbert Willis, editor of the *Fort Worth Press,* has researched and written a number of features on the subject, and generously shared his notes with the author.

J. Frank Norris' campaign against Hell's Half Acre: The only objective biography of J. Frank Norris is *Conquest or Failure,* by Ray Tatum. The book received limited circulation and attention when published in 1966; it deserved better treatment. Although it is somewhat lacking in color and presence, it is well researched and cites a wealth of sources.

IV. THE GOOD YEARS

Paddock's views: Most of the history of Fort Worth from 1872 to the turn of the century was recorded by B. B. Paddock in his lengthy, detailed histories. Yet, for interest these later, "serious" books do not match his newspaper writing in vigor. His *Early Days in Fort Worth: Much of Which I Saw and Part of Which I Was* conveys his personality intact, retaining something of his tone from his days with the *Democrat.*

Civic Improvements: The information on macadamized streets, sewers, etc., was obtained from the 1885-1886 City Directory. Other accounts give the date of "first paving" as much later, but the City Directory is so detailed in its descriptions that one finds difficulty in believing it to be in error. An insufficient base for the paving might account for the rough appearance of the streets in later photographs, and explain why later improvements were considered "first paving."

Streetcar Development: The descriptions of streetcar service and use were taken from a statement given to the *Star-Telegram* by Albert S. Leach.

V. THE AWAKENING

Aviation: The *Star-Telegram* reported in detail Roland Garros' first flight over Fort Worth, the arrival of Calbraith Perry Rodgers, and the 1915 visit of Captain Benjamin D. Foulois with the fledgling U.S. air force.

Captain Vernon Castle: The anecdote of Ely Green and Captain Vernon Castle is told in *Ely: Too Black, Too White,* one of the most moving autobiographies in existence.

Camp Bowie: The planning, development and use of Fort Worth's West Side for Army training was reported exhaustively in the *Star-Telegram.*

Oil booms: The chronology and descriptions of West Texas oil discoveries were derived chiefly from the columns of the *Star-Telegram.* Although the petroleum industry "boomed" mostly in the postwar era, research shows that, throughout most of 1918, the *Star-Telegram* devoted almost as much space to Oklahoma and Texas oil news as to the war in Europe.

BIBLIOGRAPHY

MANUSCRIPTS

Berrong, Verna E. "History of Tarrant County." M. A. Thesis, Texas Christian University, 1938.

Copeland, David. "Hell's Half Acre: Fort Worth's First Amusement Center," Texas Christian University, Research Paper, 1969, based in part on interviews with James R. Record and J. Harry Wynne.

Ferrar, Simon B. Letter to C. C. Cummings, 1893, describing founding of Fort Worth. Collection of Mrs. Catherine Terrell McCartney.

Hendricks, Delia Ann. "The Fort Worth Meat Packing Industry." Texas Christian University, Research Paper, 1969.

Texas Writers Project. *Research Data, Fort Worth and Tarrant County.* Typescript, Fort Worth Public Library. 26 vols.

NEWSPAPERS

Albuquerque Daily Democrat. 1883.

Austin Statesman. 1886.

The Civilian and Gazette Weekly (Galveston). 1860.

Daily Bulletin (Austin). 1842.

The Daily Herald (San Antonio). 1868.

Dallas Morning News. 1887.

Dallas Weekly Herald. 1876, 1884.

Fort Worth Democrat. 1873-1881.

Fort Worth Gazette. 1887.

Fort Worth Standard. 1876.

Fort Worth Star-Telegram. 1911, 1915, 1916, 1917, 1918, 1923.

San Antonio Light. 1886.

Santa Fe Daily New Mexican. 1883.

The Texas Republican (Marshall). 1849, 1854, 1855.

Texas Sentinel (Austin). 1841.

BOOKS

Abernathy, John R. *In Camp With Theodore Roosevelt, or, The Life of John R. (Jack) Abernathy.* Oklahoma City: The Times-Journal Publishing Company, 1933.

Adams, Ramon F. *Burs Under the Saddle: A Second Look at Books and Histories of the West.* Norman: University of Oklahoma Press, 1964.

Baedeker, Karl. *The United States With an Excursion into Mexico, A Handbook for Travellers.* New York: Da Capo Press, 1971 reprint of the 1893 edition.

The Book of Fort Worth. Fort Worth: The Fort Worth Record, 1913.

Cunningham, Eugene. *Triggernometry: A Gallery of Gunfighters.* Caldwell, Idaho: The Caxton Printers, 1962.

Dobie, J. Frank. *The Longhorns.* Boston: Little, Brown & Company, 1941.

Fite, Gilbert C. *The Farmers' Frontier, 1865-1900.* New York: Holt, Rinehart and Winston, Inc., 1966.

Fletcher, Baylis John. *Up the Trail in '79.* Norman: University of Oklahoma Press, 1968.

Forney, John Wier. *What I Saw in Texas.* Philadelphia: Ringwalt and Brown, 1872.

Gard, Wayne. *Rawhide Texas.* Norman: University of Oklahoma Press, 1965.
        The Chisholm Trail. Norman: University of Oklahoma Press, 1954.

Garrett, Julia Kathryn. *Fort Worth: A Frontier Triumph.* Austin: The Encino Press, 1972.

Green, Ely. *Too Black, Too White.* Ed. by Elizabeth N. & Arthur Ben Chitty. Amherst: University of Massachusetts Press, 1970.

Gruber, Frank. *The Pulp Jungle.* Los Angeles: Sherbourne Press, 1967.

Heitman, Francis B. *Historical Register and Dictionary of the United States Army, From Its Organization, September 29, 1789, to March 2, 1903.* Washington: Government Printing Office, 1903. 2 vols.

Hollon, W. Eugene and Ruth Lapham Butler (eds.). *William Bollaert's Texas.* Norman: University of Oklahoma Press, 1956.

Horan, James E. *The Wild Bunch.* New York: New American Library, 1970.

Horan, James D. & Paul Sann. *Pictorial History of the Wild West.* New York: Crown Publishers, 1954.

Hunter, J. Marvin (ed.). *The Trail Drivers of Texas.* Nashville: Cokesbury Press, 1925.

James, Marquis. *The Raven: A Biography of Sam Houston.* New York: Bobbs-Merrill Company, 1929.

Knight, Oliver. *Fort Worth, Outpost on the Trinity.* Norman: University of Oklahoma Press, 1953.

McIntire, Jim. *Early Days in Texas: A Trip to Hell and Heaven.* Kansas City, Mo.: McIntire Publishing Company, 1902.

Myres, Sandra L. (ed.). *Force Without Fanfare: The Autobiography of K. M. Van Zandt.* Fort Worth: Texas Christian University Press, 1968.

Paddock, B. B. (ed.). *A Twentieth Century History and Biographical Record of North and West Texas.* Chicago and New York: Lewis Publishing Company, 1906. 2 vols.

Paddock, B. B. *History of Texas, Fort Worth and the Texas Northwest Edition.* Chicago and New York: Lewis Publishing Company, 1922. 4 vols.

Paddock, B. B. *Early Days in Fort Worth, Much of Which I Saw and Part of Which I Was.* Fort Worth: privately published, n. d.

Preece, Harold. *Lone Star Man, Ira Aten, Last of the Old Texas Rangers.* New York: Hastings House, 1960.

Rankin, Melinda. *Texas in 1850.* Waco: Texian Press, 1966 reprint of 1850 edition.

Rodenbough, Theodore F. *From Everglades to Canyon With the Second Dragoons.* New York: D. Van Nostrand Company, 1875.

Ronnie, Art. *Locklear: The Man Who Walked on Wings.* South Brunswick and New York: A. S. Barnes and Company, 1973.

Rosa, Joseph G. *The Gunfighter, Man or Myth.* Norman: University of Oklahoma Press, 1969.

Smith, George Winston & Charles, Judah (eds.). *Chronicles of the Gringos.* Albuquerque: University of New Mexico, 1968.

Spence, Vernon Gladden. *Colonel Morgan Jones: Grand Old Man of Texas Railroading.* Norman: University of Oklahoma Press, 1971.

Stanley, F. [Stanley Francis Louis Crocchiola]. *Longhair Jim Courtright, Two Gun Marshal of Fort Worth.* Denver: World Press, 1957.

Tatum, E. Ray. *Conquest or Failure? Biography of J. Frank Norris.* Dallas: Baptist Historical Foundation, 1966.

Terrell, J. C. *Reminiscences of the Early Days of Fort Worth.* Fort Worth: Texas Printing Company, 1906.

Wilbarger, J. W. *Indian Depredations in Texas.* Austin: The Pemberton Press, 1967 reprint of the 1889 edition.

Winfrey, Dorman H. and James M. Day (ed.). *The Indian Papers of Texas and the Southwest, 1825-1916.* Austin: Pemberton Press, 1966. 5 vols.

PERIODICALS

"Burning of the Great Texas Spring Palace," *Leslie's Illustrated Newspaper,* June 14, 1890. Also June 21, 1890, page 401-407, 415; June 28, 1890, page 439.

Crimmins, M. L. (ed.). "W. F. Freemen's Report on the Eighth Military Department, 1853," *Southwestern Historical Quarterly,* LIII, No. 4, 1950.

Lipscomb, David, Comments, after visit to Fort Worth in 1872. *Gospel Advocate,* September 19, 1872.

Massad, William. "Opera Out West," *The Industrial Review,* III, No. 1, 1964.

Tyler, Ronnie C. "Quanah Parker's Narrow Escape," *Chronicles of Oklahoma,* XLVI, No. 2, 1968, 182-188.

INDEX

A

Abilene, Kansas: 34
Adams, Florence: 145
Add-Ran College. See Texas Christian University
Alexander, J. P.: 37
Alexandria, Virginia: 19
All Saints Hospital: 106
Allison, Clay: 185
Allison, Patti: 185
Alpoca Silver Mine, South America: 80
Alvarado, Texas: 72
Ambler, Emory T.: 163, 187
Ambler, Grace: 185
American Publishing Company of Milwaukee: 110
American Valley, New Mexico: 69
Anderson's, A. J., Gun Store: 87
Andrew, W. P.: 157
Anheuser-Busch Brewing Association: 94
Arion Club: 108
Arlington, Texas: 19
Arlington Heights: 140, 168
Arlington Inn: 105, 109
Armour & Co.: 107
Arnold, Brevet Major Ripley Allen: 5, 7-11, 21-22
Arnold, Sophie: 11
Arnold, Willis: 11
Audemars, Edmond: 161-162
August, A. & L., Clothing Store: 106
August, Leopold: 106
Austin, Texas 7, 15-17, 33, 71, 73-74
Austin Intelligencer: 15
Austin Statesman: 72
Automobiles. See Transportation
Aviation. See Transportation

B

Baldridge, Mrs. E. E.: 185
Ballard, Anna Hogsett: 145
Baptist Standard: 81
Barringer, J. C.: 92
Barron Field: 166, 171
Barrymore, Ethel: 109
Barrymore, John: 109
Barrymore, Lionel: 109
Bass, Sam: 67
Bateman, William: 142
Battle. See Boaz and Battle
Baylor University: 81
Beall, Ida: 61
Beaumont, Susie Bell: 145
Beckham, R. E.: 67-68
Beer Garden: 67
Belknap, Texas 18
Benbrook, Texas: 167
Benbrook Field: 171
Bernhardt, Sarah: 109
Bewley, Anthony: 16, 20
Bewley, Maisie: 145
Bicocchi, Louis, Grocery: 177
Binyon, Lola: 145
Binyon, Louise Orrick: 145
Binyon's, P. B., Transfer Office: 23
Bird's, Jonathan, Fort: 6, 9
Birdville, Texas: 9, 12-13, 15, 18
Birdville Union: 13
Birdville Western Express: 13
Blackwell, Ella: 75
Blair, Dave: 45
Blakeney, A.: 37
Boaz and Battle: 24
Boaz, David: 95
Boaz, W. J.: 37
Bon Ton: 67
Bond, Frank S.: 39
Bonita, Texas: 163
Booth, Edwin: 109
Bowie, Texas: 106, 164
Bradley, May Bell: 145
Brady, Matthew: 79
Brannan, M. M.: 43
Brazos River: 5, 8
Breckenridge, Texas: 169
Briant, E. S.: 78
Briggs, George W.: 102
Brinson, Captain M. J.: 12, 18
Broiles, H. S.: 76

Brown, Caroline: 71
Brown's Hole: 78
Brownwood, Texas: 45
Bryan, John Neely, Trading Post: 6
Buley, Anthony. See Bewley, Anthony
Burkburnett, Texas: 169
Burke, John: 132
Burleson, Colonel Edward: 6
Burnett, Samuel Burk: 60, 107-108, 124
Burr, George E.: 105, 152
Burts, Dr. W. P.: 37
Burzon, Mattie: 61
Buttermilk Junction: 71-74, 85

C

Caddo Indians: 10, 20
Calloway, Hiram: 12
Campbell, Mrs. H. H.: 62
Campbell, Harry: 62
Camp Bowie: 168-169, 190-191
Camp Bowie Base Hospital: 169
Camp Worth: 7-9
"Camp Worth," Tennessee: 19
Cantey, Sam, III: 187
Cantey, Sam B.: 155
Capps, William: 70, 155
Carlock, R. L.: 76
Carnegie, Andrew: 106
Carnegie Public Library: 176
Carroll, Rev. B. H.: 106
Carruthers Field: 166-167, 171
Carter, Amon, Sr.: 160-161, 163-165, 171, 188
Carter, Amon, Field: 171
Carter, Donnie Lee: 145
Carver, Bill: 78, 91
"Cassidy, Butch." See Parker, George Leroy
Cassidy, Mike: 77
Castle, Mrs. Irene: 167
Castle, Captain Vernon: 166-167
The Cattle Exchange (saloon): 67
Cattle industry: 33-37, 42-47, 68, 101, 107
Cattle Raisers Association of Northwest Texas: 101

Cattle Raisers Association of Texas: 101
Chamberlain, H. B., Investment Company: 105
Chapman, George: 82-83
Chase, Keating: 187
Cherokee Indians: 34
Chicago, Illinois: 34, 46
Chickamauga: 32
Children's Red Cross: 187
Chisholm, Jesse: 34
Chisholm Trail: 34, 46-47, 101
Circle Valley, Utah: 77
Cisco, Texas: 169
City-County Hospital: 106
City views. See Fort Worth
Civil War: 14-19, 25, 30-33, 66, 74, 147
Clapp: 132
Clark, Addison: 106
Clark, G. H.: 92
Clark House: 45
Clark, Ida: 106
Clark, Randolph: 106
Clay County: 18
Clear Fork, Trinity River: 5-6, 16, 35-36
Cleburne, Texas: 45
Cleveland, President Grover: 108
Cody's, Buffalo Bill, Wild West: 66
Cold Springs: 5, 9, 12, 14, 19
Cold Springs Road: 19
Colorado: 34,
Columbus, Texas: 14
Comanche Indians: 6, 10, 18, 20, 34, 101-102, 109, 124
Concho River: 45
Confederate Home for Men: 114
Connell, W. E.: 157
Cooke County: 18
Corning, A. F.: 18
Courthouse. See Tarrant County Courthouse
Courtney, John J.: 13
Courtright, T. I., Commercial Detective Agency: 69
Courtright, Marshal Timothy Isaiah "Long Hair Jim": 64-76, 84
Courtright, Betty: 66, 70, 76
Cowart, Robert E.: 38
Cox, John: 143

Crafton, Texas: 164
Crawford, Mr.: 16, 20
Creek Indians: 34
Cromer, H. R.: 170
Cross Timbers: 5
Crucifixion of Sally: 76
Cultural pursuits: 74, 97, 100, 103, 106-109
Curry, "Flat-Nosed George": 79

D

Dade, Dabney C.: 12
Daggett, C. B.: 11, 22
Daggett, Captain Eph: 11-14, 17, 20, 22, 33, 36
Daggett, Henry: 10-11, 22
Dallas, Texas: 6-7, 11-13, 16, 38, 42-43, 46, 73, 79, 81, 104
Dallas-Fort Worth Spurs: 133
Dallas Herald: 18, 38-39, 42-43, 47, 68-69
Dallas Morning News: 76
Dallas News: 71
Darnell, Nicholas H.: 41
Davis, Jennie Walker: 145
Davis, Jim: 132
Davis, Lillie: 78
Davis, W. D.: 83
Day, Mayor G. H.: 42, 68
Decatur, Texas: 45
De Crasse, Joseph: 109
Denison, Texas: 72, 163
Denton, Texas: 16
Denver, Colorado: 78, 80, 85
Desdemona, Texas: 169
De Young's: 79
Diltz: 132
Dimaio, Frank: 79-80, 85
Doan's Store: 44
Dobie, J. Frank: 107
Dockstader, Lew, Minstrels: 108
Dodge City, Kansas: 75
Doyle, W. J.: 142
Driver's Club: 162
Driving Park: 161, 170
Dugan, H.: 28

Duke, Joe: 169
Dunlap, Judge O. E.: 166-167
Durbin, Corp. J. W.: 92
Duringer, Dr. W. A.: 128
Duringer, Mrs. (W. A.): 128
Duse, Elenora: 109

E

Eagle Ford, Texas: 38-40, 67
Earp, Wyatt: 75
Easley, James Daniel: 141, 143
Eastland, Texas: 169
Edgington, J. E.: 143
Edrington, Eva: 149
Educational facilities: 11, 81, 100, 106, 139-145, 176
Elgin Watch Factory Band: 103-104
Ellis Hotel: 51
El Paso Hotel: 45
Elsing, Robert: 69
Elysian Fields, Texas: 32
Evans Hall: 100
Everman Field: 171

F

Fairbanks, Douglas: 109
Fairmont Addition: 102
Fakes & Company: 87
Famous Shoe Store: 158
Farmer, John Press: 9, 12, 20, 22
Farmer, Sue: 20
Farmers Branch, Texas: 6
Farnum, Dustin: 108
Fat Stock Show: 80, 124
Feild, Julian B.: 11-13
Feild, Dr. Julian Theodore: 111, 128
Feild, Mrs. Julian T.: 128
Feild, Mary (of Fort Worth): 136, 149
Feild, Mary (of Denison): 149
Feild, Willie: 149
Fenderick, Charles: 4
Ferrar, Simon B.: 5

Fields, Ann: 145
Fire stations: 49, 101
First Baptist Church of Fort Worth: 81, 96
First National Bank: 157
Flatiron Building: 153
Fletcher, Baylis John: 68
Forney, John Weiss: 35-36, 47
Fort Arbuckle, Oklahoma: 34, 46
Fort Belknap, 11, 45
Fort Concho (San Angelo): 45
Fort Donelson, Tennessee: 66
Fort Graham: 7-8, 11
Fort Griffin: 43-45
Fort Griffin Echo: 45
Fort Parker: 6, 18
Fort Sam Houston: 165
Fort Worth:
    city views of, frontispiece, 86
    economic conditions, 31, 33-35, 37-39, 42,
        44, 46, 99-100, 106, 108, 170
    established, 5
    founding of, 5-11
    incorporation of, 37
    military in, 5-11, 19, 21, 165-169, 171, 188-191
    origin of name, 4, 7
    population, 11-15, 18-19, 31, 34-36, 38,
        41, 44, 46, 107, 164, 170
Fort Worth Advertising Club: 165
Fort Worth-Birdville feud: 12-13, 15
Fort Worth Cats: 133
Fort Worth Chief: 15
Fort Worth Club: 132
Fort Worth-Dallas Interurban: 125-126
Fort Worth Democrat: 37, 40-45, 47, 68, 100-101, 128
Fort Worth and Denver City House: 23
Fort Worth & Denver City Railroad: 164
Fort Worth Dressed Meat and Packing Company: 107
Fort Worth Elks Club: 165
Fort Worth Fencibles: 108, 127
Fort Worth Gazette: 73-74
Fort Worth High School: 139
Fort Worth International Airport: 171
Fort Worth-Jacksboro Stage Line: 15

Fort Worth Land and Investment Company: 110
Fort Worth Mandolin Club: 135
Fort Worth National Bank: 30, 39, 58
Fort Worth Opera House: 108, 137
Fort Worth Press: 85
Fort Worth Public Library Association: 106
Fort Worth Record: 82, 108, 124
Fort Worth and Rio Grande Railroad: 52
Fort Worth Standard: 43-45, 67
Fort Worth Star: 164, 172
Fort Worth Star-Telegram: 85, 161, 163, 165, 169, 172
Fort Worth Stockyards: 123, 125
Fort Worth Telegram: 164, 172
Fort Worth Traction Company: 125-126
Fort Worth University: 106, 109, 141-143
Fosdick, Plenny: 141
Foulois, Captain Benjamin D.: 165-166, 171, 188
Fowler, A. Y.: 12
Fowler, S. L.: 169
Frank Leslie's Illustrated Newspaper: 14, 104-105, 152
Freeman, Colonel W. G.: 21
French, W. L. (photographer): 178

G

Gahagan, H. T.: 157
Galveston, Texas: 71
Gambling: 76. See also Law and Order
Garros, Roland G.: 162, 170, 186
Ginnochio Hotel: 70
Goodfellows Fund: 165
Gould, Jay: 71
Graham Brothers Grocery Store: 154, 181
Grapevine: 17
Grapevine Prairie: 6
Gray, Eunice. See Place, Etta
Great Northern Railroad: 79
Green, Ely: 166-167
Greenwall's Opera House: 103, 108
Greenwood Cemetery: 171
Griffith, Alberta: 145
Grimes, Lieutenant A. C.: 92
Grossette, Alexander: 69
Guthrie, Jack: 187

H
Hall, Captain J. Lee: 101
Hancock, Mr. Joel: 40
Hanks, Deaf Charley: 78
Harney, General William S.: 7
Harris, Abe: 10
Harrison County: 32
Harrold, Texas: 73, 102
Hayne, Al. S.: 105, 152
Hayne, Al. S., monument: 109, 173
The Headlight Bar: 66
Helena, Montana: 79
Hell's Half Acre: 2, 65, 67-68, 76-78, 80-82, 84-85, 96
Hendricks, Judge H. G.: 36
Hickock, James Butler "Wild Bill": 66
Hicks Field: 171
Hirsch Lake. See Hurst Lake
Hirsch Lake Art Club. See Hurst Lake Art Club
Hodge, Texas: 72, 85
Hogsett, Judge J. Y.: 37, 54-55
Hogsett, Cora: 137
Hogsett, Ella: 145
Hogsett, Mrs. Joe B.: 187
Hogtown, Texas. See Desdemona, Texas
"Hole in the Wall Gang": 77-78
Hollingsworth, Grace Gant: 145
Honea, B. N.: 164
Hood County: 106
Hornbeak, W. A.: 56
Horse Head (saloon): 67
Houston, Sam: 13-15, 17
Houston, Texas: 38-39, 78
Humphreys, Clifton: 141
Hunter, H.: 132
Hurst Lake: 128, 131
Hurst Lake Art Club: 128, 131
Hutchins Hotel: 23

I
Indian Nations: 34-35
Indian Territory: 60, 175
Indian Wars: 66
Ireland, John: 73-74
Isbell, Paul: 14, 16

J
Jack County: 18
Jacksboro, Texas: 37, 45
James Brothers: 77
James, Hatcher: 135
Jarrott, Mrs. Mollie: 164
Jarvis, J. J.: 39
Jennings, Thomas: 115
Johnson County: 72
Johnson (North), Miss Floy: 185
Johnson, Mrs. J. Lee: 185
Johnson, Jake: 75-76
Johnson, M. T., Hook and Ladder Company: 37, 40, 66
Johnson, Tom: 12, 132
Johnson, Colonel Middleton Tate: 5, 17-18
Johnson's Station: 5, 14, 19
Johnston, Abbie: 145

K
Kansas: 34, 44
Kasan, Billy: 170
Keeler, Mrs. D. B.: 106
Ketchum, "Blackjack" (Tom): 78-79
Ketchum, Sam: 78-79
Kibbie, Dr. Kent: 142
"Kid Curry." See Logan, Harvey
Kilpatrick, Ben: 78, 91
King brothers: 31
King, Richard: 120
King, W. B.: 52
Kiowa Indians: 6, 20, 101, 124
Knights of Labor: 71-73
Ku Klux Klan: 33
Kuhley, Charles: 92
Kussatz, Herman: 67

L
Lake Chalco: 7
Lake Como: 105
Lake Como Casino: 138
Lake Erie: 138
Lake Valley, New Mexico Territory: 68-69
Lake Worth, Texas: 168-169

Lake Worth, Florida: 19
Lane, W. P.: 83
Langtry, Lilly: 109
La Shell, Kirk: 108
Lauder, Harry: 109
Lay, Elza: 78-79
Leach, Albert S.: 102
Leach, H. S.: 102
Leadville, Colorado: 75
Leigh, Charles Wilburn: 142
Leonard, Archibald F.: 10, 11, 16, 20
Leonard, Marvin: 171
Leslie, Frank: 104-105
Lewis, Henry: 163, 171
Limestone County: 9
Linsky, David: 53
Literary Society: 109
Lloyd Rifles: 108
Locklear, Ormer: 167, 171
Logan, Harvey ("Kid Curry"): 78-79, 91
Logan, General John Alexander: 66, 69
Logan, Lonny: 79
Lonesome Dove: 6
Longbaugh, Harry ("The Sundance Kid"): 78-80, 85, 91
"Long Hair Jim." See Courtright, Marshal Timothy Isaiah
López de Santa Anna, Antonio de: 12-13
"Jim Lowe." See Parker, George Leroy
Loyd, Greene: 157
Loyd, Martin B.: 37, 45, 47, 157
Loyd's Exchange Office: 46
Lusk, John P.: 6

M
McCall, M. D.: 37
McCarty gang: 77
McCarty, Tom: 77
McCleskey, John: 169
McCoy, Joseph G.: 33-34
McIntire, Jim: 69-71
McLean, Jeff: 80
McLennan County: 150
Mabry, Major Seth: 43

Mackenzie, Colonel Ranald S.: 20
Madame Centz' Female Minstrels: 67
Maddox Flats: 78
Maddox, Walter: 70, 73
Malone, Mary: 61
Mandolin Club: 109
Mansion: 45
Marine Creek: 70
Marlin, Thomas P.: 135
Marrow Bone Creek. See Mary le Bone Creek
Marshall, Texas: 8, 14
Martin, Mr. (science teacher): 141
Martin, R. C.: 157
Mary le Bone Creek: 19
Mary's Creek: 67
Masonic Temple: 20
Massengale, W. R.: 34
Massey, Dallas: 157
Masterson, Bat: 75
Mathewson, William (Buffalo Bill): 34
Mayes, L. C.: 157
Meacham, H. C.: 106
Merchant's Restaurant: 71
Metropolitan Hotel: 165, 188
Mexican War: 4, 6, 11
Mexico: 6
Mexico City: 6
Missionary Ridge: 32
Missouri-Kansas-Texas Railroad station: 175
Missouri Pacific Railroad: 72
Mock, Mr.: 31
Moisant, John B.: 161
Monnig's: 106
Monnig, George: 106
Monnig, William: 106
Montague County: 18
Montgomery, Tommie: 145
Montgomery Ward: 170, 186
Moody, Captain Thomas A.: 18
Moore, Dr. H. W.: 100
Moore, Malcolm: 135
Moore, Stuart: 132
Morgan, John C.: 66

Morris, Chief Justice J. S.: 40
Morrison, Pat: 90
Morse, D. D.: frontispiece
Morton, Mr.: 142
Mullett: 132

N
Nace, Thomas: 74
Navarro County: 9
Nebraska: 34
"New Chisum" Trail. See Chisolm Trail
New Mexico Territory: 68-69, 71, 79
Newman, A. T.: 142
Newspapers: 8, 13-15, 18, 20, 35-39, 41-45,
　47, 67-69, 71-74, 76, 81, 100, 104, 107-108, 124,
　128, 161-162, 164-165, 169, 172
Neye, Fred, 141, 143
Nicholson, A. P.: 132
Nobby Harness Company: 179
Norman, Oklahoma: 164
Norris, Rev. J. Frank: 81-84, 96
North, Miss Floy Johnson. See Johnson (North), Miss Floy
North, J. M., Jr.: 164
North, Mrs. James: 185
North Side Coliseum: 82, 124
Norton, Anthony Banning: 15-17
Norvell Corset Shop: 184

O
Oakley, Annie: 66
Oakwood Cemetery: 84
The Occidental (saloon): 66
Oil Industry: 169-170
O'Keefe, Gussie: 185
Oklahoma: 164
Oklahoma City University: 141
Oklahoma Territory: 107
Old Fiddler's contest: 121
Operas: 100, 103, 108, 137
Our Comrades (saloon): 67

Our Friends (saloon): 67
Owens, Will: 92

P
Pacific Hotel: 45
Paddock, Captain Buckley B.: 1, 22, 36-47, 52,
　98-100, 104-105, 107, 109, 112, 129
Paddock, William: 112
Palestine, Texas: 72, 78
Palo Pinto County: 18
Panic of 1837: 32
Panic of 1873: 37-39
Panic of 1893: 108
"Panther City": 38, 43
Paris, Texas: 163
Parker, Cynthia Ann: 18, 109
Parker, Dan: 120
Parker, George Leroy: 77-80, 85, 91
Parker, Isaac: 18
Parker, Prairie Flower: 18
Parker, Quanah: 18, 60, 101-102, 109, 124
Parker, Silas: 18
Parker County: 17-18
Peak, Dr. Carroll M.: 12, 20
Peak, Howard W.: 20, 43, 120
Pease River: 18
Peta Nocona: 18, 109
Peters Land Company: 6
Peterson, Colonel R. 163
Philadelphia Press: 35
Pickett, Sam: 92
Pickwick Hotel: 102
Pierce, Frank: 74
Pilot Point, Texas: 16
Pinkerton, William: 78, 85
Pinkerton Detective Agency: 78-80, 85
Pioneer Rest Cemetery: 11
Pitner, Virgile: 61
Place, Etta: 78-80, 85
Plains Indians: 6, 20, 101
Polytechnic College: 144

Porter, Fannie: 78-79, 85
Porter, Tony: 56
Potter, Grace: 145
Portwood, Bill: 187
Powder Springs: 77
Prairie Flower (Parker). See Parker, Prairie Flower
Pummill, J. L., Meat Market and Delicatessen: 178
Purvis, Ned: 16
Putts, Henry: 92

Q

Quayle, William: 17
"Queen City of the Prairies": 86
Quitman Herald: 37

R

Railroads. See Transportation
Railroad strike of 1886: 72-74, 92
Randol Mill Road: 20
Randol, W. A.: 20
Ranger Texas: 169
Record, James R.: 164
The Red Light (saloon): 67, 84
Red River: 44, 101
Regan Millinery Shop: 183
Remington, Frederic: 51
Republic of Texas: 6, 30
Reynolds, Betty: 185
Rhau, Conrad: 136
Rhine (photographer): 150
Richards, William A.: 77
Richardson, Mr.: 143
Richmond, Adah, English Opera Troupe: 100
Richmond, Harry: 70-71
Riley, Jim: 132
Riverside: 81
Robber's Roost: 78
Robinson, J. R.: 92
Rodgers, Calbraith Perry "Daredevil Cal": 163-164, 186
Roosevelt, President Theodore: 107, 175-176
Root, Miss Stella: 131

Ross, Jennie: 185
Ross, Captain Lawrence Sullivan: 18
Roy, J. W.: 40
Royal Flying Corps of Canada: 166-167
Runnels, Governor Hardin R.: 13-14
Rusk, General Thomas J.: 84, 88
Russell, Lillian: 79, 109
Ryan pasture: 163, 165, 171, 186, 188
Ryan Place Addition: 171

S

St. Joseph's Hospital: 106
Saloons: 56, 66-67, 74-75, 78, 84
Sally. See Crucifixion of Sally
Samuels, Annie: 145
San Angelo, Texas: 45
San Antonio, Texas: 6-7, 165-166
San Antonio Daily Herald: 20
San Antonio Light: 74
San Jacinto: 13, 84
Santa Anna. See López de Santa Anna, Antonio de
Santa Fe Railroad: 73
Saunders, George W.: 35
Schmitt, Capt. G. H.: 92
Scott, Colonel Thomas A.: 35-36
Scott, General Winfield: 7
Scott, Winfield: 108
Seminole Indian Wars: 6-7
Shawnee Trail: 46
Sherman Register: 39
Short, Luke: 64, 74-76
Shreveport, Louisiana: 33
Sierra Mining Company: 69
Simon, Rene: 162
Slack, Ora Stroud: 145
Slack, T. W.: 157
Slaughter, George: 12
Slavery: 13-14
Smith, George: 15
Smith, John Peter: 11, 17-18, 22, 39, 73-74
Smith, Karl: 108
Smith, Lillian: 66

Sneed, Charlie: 73
Sonora: 78
Southwestern Baptist Theological Seminary: 106, 168
Spanish-American War: 108
Spring Palace. See Texas Spring Palace
Stag Saloon: 56
"Statue of Liberty": 162
Steele, Lawrence: 13, 20
"Steele's Tavern": 13, 15
Steiner, Dr. Josephus M.: 11
Stone and Webster: 126
Storms, Charley: 75
Stove Foundry Road: 168-169
Streetcars. See Transportation
Stripling, Lucy: 185
Stripling, W. C.: 106
Stubbs, Nat: 132
"The Sundance Kid." See Longbaugh, Harry
Sunset, Texas: 164
Swartz, Charles L.: 120, 131, 145
Swartz, D. H.: 117
Swift & Co.: 107
Sycamore Creek: 41-42

T

Tagliapietra Grand Italian Opera Company: 100
Taliaferro Field: 166-167, 171
Tandy, Annie: 141
Tankersley, Elmore: 142
"Tarantula Map": 37, 45
Tarlton, Francis: 145
Tarrant County: 9, 12, 16-18, 68, 101, 106
Tarrant County Construction Company: 39-40
Tarrant County Courthouse: 15, 19, 25, 31,
    40-41, 44, 106, 117, 118-119
Tarrant County General Pastor's Association: 82
Tarrant, General Edward H.: 6, 9
Taylor, Colonel Holman: 168
Taylor, General Zachary: 6
Taylor, May: 185
Telluride, Colorado: 77
Tenmey, J. M.: 157

Terrell, Captain Ed: 6, 19, 120
Terrell, E. S.: 37
Terrell, J. C.: 12, 120
Terrell, John J.: 143
Terrell, Josie: 141
Terrell, Sue: 61
Terry, Colonel Nathaniel: 12, 14
Texas Advertising and Manufacturing Company: 164
Texas and Pacific Railway Company: 35-36, 38-41,
    67, 93, 152
Texas and Pacific Railway Station: 44, 48, 107,
    116, 148, 151, 174
T & P (Texas and Pacific) Reservation: 45, 103-104
Texas & Pacific Union Station: 173
Texas Christian University: 106, 141, 145
Texas Flower Parade and Festival: 148-149
Texas Rangers: 8, 15, 18, 69-70, 73
Texas Rangers (baseball team): 133
Texas Republican: 8, 14
Texas Revolution: 6, 88
Texas Spring Palace: 103-105, 110, 150-152
Texas Wesleyan University: 106, 141
Theater Comique: 65, 67
Thompson, Mrs. Julia: 79
Thorp Springs: 45, 106, 145
Throckmorton, Governor J. W.: 35
Tidball, Thomas A.: 39
Tidball, Van Zandt, and Company.
    See Fort Worth National Bank
Tivoli Hall: 87
Tivoli Saloon: 66-67
Tombstone, Arizona: 75
Tomlinson, William: 80
Tonkawa Indians: 10, 20
Toronto, Canada: 71
Towash, Chief: 10
Towash village: 7
Townsond, Dick: 73
Tracy, Harry: 78
Transcontinental Hotel: 45
Transportation:
    aviation, 161-171, 186, 188-189
    automobiles, 163, 187, 192

railroad, frontispiece, 35-36, 38-43, 45-46, 48, 52,
   67-68, 71-74, 79, 92-93, 101, 105, 164, 173-175
stagecoaches, 13, 15, 44-46
streetcars, 44, 102, 105, 122, 126, 176, 192
wagons, 11-13
Trimble, Mary Lou: 141
Trimble, John "Blinkie": 135
Trinity River: 1, 5-6, 8-9, 13, 19, 35, 44, 67, 70, 100, 105
Trinity (saloon): 67
Triplett, S. D.: 157
Tucker: 12
Turner, Charles: 12, 14
Turner, W. G.: 28
Twentieth Street Drug Store: 182

U

Union Depot: 73
Union Pacific Railroad: 78

V

Van Zandt, Isaac: 30, 32
Van Zandt, Major Khleber Miller: 1, 25, 30-32, 36-39, 46
Van Zandt County: 18
Vicksburg, Mississippi: 66
Virginia City, Nevada: 66
Virginia House (hotel): 45

W

Wabash Railway Company: 71
Waco, Texas: 82, 106, 145
Waco Hotel: 85
Waco Tap: 66
Waco Village: 7
Waggoner, Tom: 107-108
Wagner, Montana: 79
Waldo Quintette: 135
Walker, A. G.: 13
Walker, Maud: 78
Walkup, James A.: 180
Walla Walla, Washington Territory: 71

Waller, Mary: 145
War of 1812: 6
Washer Brothers: 57, 106
Washer, Jacob: 106
Washer, Nat: 106
Washington, D. C.: 19
Washington Territory: 71
Waxahachie, Texas: 16, 166
Weatherford, Texas: 17, 18, 45, 67
Webster. See Stone and Webster
Weeks, Sarah Elizabeth. See Courtright, Betty
Wellge, Henry: 110
West Fork, Trinity River: 5, 35-36
Westbrook Hotel: 167, 169, 184
"Western Trail": 44
Westland Cigar Manufacturing Company: 156
Westover Hills: 169
The White Elephant: 67, 74-75
White Settlement: 12, 16, 20
White Settlement Road: 161, 169
White, Thomas R.: 141, 143
Whitesboro, Texas: 163
Whiting, Lieutenant William H. C.: 9
Wichita County: 169
Wichita Falls, Texas: 70
Wichita Indians: 8, 102
Wichita Mountains, Arkansas Territory: 8
Wigfall, Louis T.: 13
"Wild Bunch": 78-80, 85
Wiley: 143
Williamson, Frances: 185
Wilson, John: 39
Wing, Mr.: 143
Winston, Thomas: 157
Wire Bridge: 119
Wise County: 12, 18, 164
Withers, M. A.: 34
Women's Humane Society: 173
Wood, Dickson, Mercantile Company: 50
Wood, Governor George T.: 9
Wood, T. J.: 80
Woody, A. W.: 69-70
Woody, Captain Sam: 12, 120

World War I: 1, 165, 167, 170-171, 189-190
World War I Fliers Club: 171
Worth, General William Jenkins: 4, 6-7, 19
Worth Hotel: 103, 107
Wortham, Louis J.: 164
Wynne, Colonel Richard M.: 113-114

X
Xray: 84

Y
Yellow Bear: 101-102
York, Sheriff John B.: 12
Young County: 18
Younger Brothers: 77

Book design and production: RYA/Crawford Dunn, Incorporated, Dallas

Typographic composition: Southwestern Typographics Inc., Dallas

Lithography: Steck-Warlick Company, Austin, Dallas, Houston

Binding: Universal Bookbindery, Inc., San Antonio

Type faces: Linofilm Helvetica; running heads, 24-point light; text, 9 on 13 with 30-point bold initial; quotations, 8 on 11 light; backmatter, 8 on 11 with bold; captions, 7 on 8; cover, Techni-Process Helvetica TH10 with TH07

Cover: Joanna Western's Arrestox C-31500 book cloth, Brown, on .080 binding board with hot-stamped white title

End paper: Champion's, 80 lb., Chalice Opaque Vellum, white

Text paper: Westvaco's, 80 lb., Sterling Dull, white

Dust jacket: Champion's, 80 lb., Wedgewood Gloss, white

Binding method: Smyth-sewn with drawn-on cover